MW00941419

FIGHTING
SICKNESS
WITH
FITNESS

HARMONIZING YOUR MIND, BODY & SPIRIT
TO LIVE A HEALTHIER AND HAPPIER LIFE

JUSTIN YANAGIDA

This book is dedicated to my family in Japan—my mother, Tomoyo Yanagida, my father, James Yanagida, and my fiancée, Jodi Ann Tomooka. I love you guys and thank you for supporting me from the beginning.

Disclaimer

The health and/or nutritional information included in this book is not intended to be a substitute for medical advice, diagnosis, or treatment by a doctor. Always seek the advice of your physician with any questions you may have regarding a medical condition. Never disregard medical advice or delay seeking it because of something you have read in this program. We release the writer from any and all liability by reading on.

Table of Contents

Foreword

I know as well as anyone that you can fight sickness through fitness. In fact, I actually started my business, Fitness Quest 10, because of a health setback. After graduating from William and Mary, I played pro football in Europe. During one game I suffered a severe back injury, suffering three herniated discs and getting diagnosed with degenerative back disease and spinal stenosis.

Laying on the field that day, I watched my dreams of becoming a professional quarterback in the NFL disappear. I was devastated, but at the same time, I was determined to get better. For several years after that, I searched for ways to heal myself. I reached out to anyone who could help me including doctors, massage therapists, specialists in Rolfing, Feldenkrais practitioners, physical therapists, trainers, acupuncturists, osteopaths, and even Reiki healers. Ultimately, not only did I get myself better, I ended up opening a business to help others get better as well.

FOREWORD

In 20+ years of owning my business, thousands of people have come to me asking how to lose weight. What I have learned is that it isn't always the number on the scale that they're after. What they really want is to feel better, to be happier and to live a healthier life.

You see, getting healthy is not about just your weight on the scale. Being healthy actually starts on the inside with mindset and exercise. If you're not addressing those, then it doesn't matter how much you weigh on the scale, how much money you have, what career you pursue, or anything else. As Steven Adler says, "You can have all the riches and success in the world, but if you don't have your health, you have nothing."

That's why I am so pumped about this book. Not only has Justin based his entire business on the idea that healing comes from the inside out, he has now put it all down on paper. In these pages, you are going to learn the exact system he uses to get people healthy. If you want to live a happier, healthier life, then this book is going to help you get there. That fires me up!

I have known Justin for a few years now, and he is one of the most passionate fit pros I have ever met. His smile lights up the room, and he has devoted his life to helping people get better. He truly is a lighthouse and with this book, he is shining his light a little further out into the world.

If you're ready to live a healthier, happier life, then enjoy this book and share it with others. One person at a time, we can fire up the universe and create IMPACT!

Get strong mentally and physically...and go be a LIGHT!

Peace, love, and lots of great health,

Todd Durkin, MA, CSCS
Owner, Fitness Quest 10
Under Armour Training Team
Head Coach, Todd Durkin Mastermind Program
Author, ***The IMPACT Body Plan*** and ***The WOW Book***

Introduction

If you picked up this book wondering if this is just another fitness book with generic exercises and over-complicated diet plans with insane restrictions, I'm here to assure you that it's not. Instead, I created this book as a testament to healthy living, both for myself and for those around me.

My parents moved to Hawaii from Japan before I was born. We did not have a lot of money and sometimes ate what we could to get by. Growing up with the trials and tribulations that come with being an immigrant family, I have learned so much. Besides growing up and learning English as a second language, I was also born with a liver problem and had horrible asthma attacks up until high school. At one point, I weighed 40 pounds over my recommended weight and was diagnosed with ADHD. Because of my health struggles, I feel fortunate to be able to empathize and show compassion to my team and clients by working with them to develop stronger bodies, hearts, and minds.

Health is not limited to the physical but also includes mental and emotional health, something I came to realize as a teenager. At that time in my life, I had been bullied and battered for over a year and felt alone with no friends or support. In an act of desperation and hopelessness, I walked up to a bridge, closed my eyes, and lifted one foot in the air, ready to end my pain and suffering. In that fleeting moment, I saw the faces of my family members and recalled the dreams that I had of becoming a fitness professional and serving the world. I put my foot down and opened my eyes. Right then and there, I decided that I was going to learn everything I could to improve myself to make that dream a reality.

Soon after, a family friend asked me to join her family's martial arts class to learn self-defense and Brazilian Jiu Jitsu from her husband, Keith Inouye. I started attending classes regularly and my confidence rose. I joined the high school's wrestling team because I wanted to see how things could be different with this new self-confidence. However, one of the boys at school seemed to notice this change. We were in the wrestling room before practice, waiting for our coaches to arrive. He decided that my newfound confidence was somehow a threat to him, and he began to provoke me with teasing and name-calling like he did in the past. I positioned myself in front of him, not letting what he said get under my skin. Before I knew it, he charged at my legs, slamming me down into the mat. I quickly realized what was happening and defended myself using the only technique I knew I could use in a disadvantaged position, the triangle choke. Within seconds of locking on the choke, he began begging me to let go. We got up, and he looked at me in shock and with the respect that no bully had ever showed me before. I was never bullied again after that.

After the first few weeks of training in Jiu Jitsu, I realized that I would need much more strength and conditioning training if I wanted to be competitive in the sport. I was barely able to do 10 push-ups in a row and had difficulty doing a single pull-up. I signed up for an old-school iron gym over the beautiful air-conditioned fitness center because I loved how hard most of the people trained in the environment. However, I was also highly intimidated by these people and only went to the gym once or twice a week. I trained on my own, not knowing what I was doing, and ended up hurting myself multiple times. I hurt my rotator cuff and lower back using too much weight with improper form. During the weeks that I avoided the gym I would study any material I could get my hands on regarding exercises and fitness. This also led me to find another aspect of health, recovery, which was at the time self-myofascial release. Currently I'll implement many recovery protocols from self-myofascial release, hand-held percussion gun, cold water therapy and deep tissue massage.

I became obsessed with learning from different sources and fitness experts and made a commitment to work very hard to improve myself so that one day I could help others. I continued to train in college, only doing half of what I did in high school, before giving in to the temptations of alcohol. One day after a party, I felt sharp pains in my liver. I had it checked by a local doctor, only to be told that due to my pre-existing liver condition, even having one-two drinks a week could massively flare up my liver. If I did not stop, I would be on track for liver cirrhosis and cancer. I took the news very hard for a few weeks, knowing that if I didn't change, I would shorten my life significantly. I stopped drinking alcohol completely and got back into my regular fitness routine. I dedicated myself fully to strength training and Brazilian Jiu-Jitsu training, learning from a Rickson Gracie black belt, Romolo Barros.

This was the first time in months that I had been eating well, sleeping well, and training on a daily basis. By the time the year had gone by, I saw the results of my hard work and had a renewed passion for health and fitness. With this new desire to help others, I dropped out of college and flew 6,000 miles away from everything familiar to attend one of the best personal training trade schools in the States, the National Personal Training Institute.

When I arrived, I was blessed with having some of the best teachers and mentors, Luis Lopez and Chris Williams. During my time there, I was introduced to many different modalities of training and eating for different goals, bodies, and various circumstances. From the hundreds of hours of hands-on training, I began to realize that I had been right. This was my calling and a vehicle to serve. I started to believe that I could make a change in other people's lives, not only in my home state of Hawaii, but also around the world.

Since then, I have had the opportunity to train and serve thousands of people, including middle school students, professional athletes, people with busy schedules such as managers and stay-at-home mothers, and grandparents who have grandkids to babysit. I have worked with many types of people with various backgrounds, all of which require a different strategy to achieve freedom in their health and fitness.

What You Will Not Find

In this book, you will not find a cookie-cutter, one-size-fits-all program, nor will you find grand claims, such as losing 50 pounds in four weeks, both of which are heavily promoted in today's fitness market.

Fighting Sickness with Fitness will empower you to take control of your life by educating positive habits that last much longer than following a generic program. In the following chapters, I will show you a customizable blueprint for developing your life through fitness in all areas: physical, emotional, and mental. The methodologies in this book are what we practice and preach to our clients who have lowered their blood markers and lost upwards of 60 pounds in a year. I truly hope that you read and reread this book and use the stories and methodologies to help you on your journey to reaching your full potential.

CHAPTER 1

What is Fighting Sickness with Fitness?

Fighting Sickness with Fitness is a message, utilizing fundamental exercise, diet, and recovery habits to combat and overcome health issues rather than relying on medication. Formerly inhaling, swallowing, and injecting medications, I can tell you first-hand that many medications can cause us to lose so much of our energy, enthusiasm, and creativity. Although I do understand that there are certain conditions and illnesses that require modern medicine, the growing epidemics of obesity, Type 2 diabetes, high blood pressure, and high cholesterol can be prevented and possibly reversed through proper diet, exercise, and rest.

Back when I did not know any better, I trained purely for cosmetic reasons while sacrificing my health and well-being. I ate processed foods, worked out six days a week, and slept only 4-5 hours a night. Remembering my experiences and watching many of my clients, I know that when we focus on health, our body composition improves even without watching our food intake and meticulously counting calories.

When I first made the shift to working out for health and performance, I had to make a commitment and take immediate action in my life so that the training and eating habits would become my daily habits. After a few months of self-motivation, the training and nutrition habits started to become second nature. It was almost awkward if I didn't do it and veered off course. When I did, it felt like skipping a shower or forgetting to brush your teeth.

Fighting Sickness with Fitness, or FSF, does not mean that you are doing insane amounts of high-intensity weight lifting or cross training every day, nor does it mean that the food you eat has to be dry and flavorless. It is simply making a commitment to yourself to strive for great health so that you can maintain a high level of energy, creativity, and passion for yourself and your loved ones.

Fighting Sickness with Fitness is much more than physical fitness. It's a way of life. We can all improve our mental, spiritual, and emotional levels of fitness because when neglected they can make us become ill. Striving to reach our full potential requires a fit mind, body, and spirit. The only way we can achieve fitness and not fixes in these areas is to continually overcome challenges, learn, and practice discipline and consistency.

I had the privilege of connecting with and interviewing people I admire and believe are fit physically, mentally, and emotionally. Here are the habits and qualities they all had in common:

Habits and Qualities of Those Physically Fit

- Exercises daily (walking, running, resistance training, yoga, tai chi, etc.)

- Eats wholesome, natural food most of the time and enjoys an occasional treat

- Drinks a gallon of water a day

- Sleeps six-nine hours a day

- Incorporates recovery methods (mobility, flexibility, soft tissue work, etc.)

Habits and Qualities of Those Mentally Fit

– Self-educates at least 30 minutes a day (books, audio books, podcasts, etc.)

– Believes we all have unlimited potential

– Strives to add value and serve others

– Is surrounded by smarter, faster, and wiser individuals

– Commits to completing their responsibilities

– Remains coachable with an open mind, willing to try creative and challenging things

– Attends conferences, seminars, and additional training

– Embraces challenges as opportunities

– Always takes responsibility for shortcomings and mistakes

– Understands that the best investment is in themselves

Habits and Qualities of Those Emotionally Fit

– Practices gratitude daily

– Practices humility and admits shortcomings and mistakes

- Believes that things happen through us for the benefit of others
- Forgives and wishes others well
- Employs empathy, encouragement, and empowerment to others
- Listens to understand and not simply to respond
- Sets special time aside for family and loved ones

I truly believe that we should all strive to be fit and healthy regardless of our age, conditions, and circumstances. With all the things going on in the world today, I have not seen or heard anybody tell me that they are not busy. Whether you are 60 years old with various conditions, a very busy stay-at-home parent with many obligations, or a manager who works 60+ hours a week, I promise you that it is possible to make that change.

Resistance Training

Resistance training is any type of exercise that utilizes resistance using our own body weight, free-weight or weight machines to achieve muscular contractions, which build the strength, size, and endurance of our muscles depending on the workout parameters. Some little-known benefits include injury prevention and bone strengthening, which reduces the risk of osteoporosis. A recent study also showed that strength training at least once a week for half an hour reduces the risk of heart disease. I want to go over the basic fundamentals that will help build the foundation of your fitness. None of these principles are revolutionary, which is why they are called fundamentals.

Multi-joint movements such as squats, lunges, presses, rows, and deadlifts will yield the best results. Gradually building up strength in those movements will massively improve your quality of life and dependence on others. Nearly all multi-joint movements are functional and practical for everyday activities from gardening, playing with the kids, hauling groceries, moving furniture, and many other life activities that require stronger muscles and joints. Single joint isolation movements do have their place and, depending on your situation and goals, may be implemented into your program. They can be highly beneficial but should not be the focus of the workout.

Cardiovascular

The American Heart Association (AHA) recommends performing 150 minutes of moderate intensity or 75 minutes of high intensity a week to gain the overall cardiovascular benefits. AHA also recommends including at least two days of strength training for additional health benefits.

With any new goal or endeavor, it is always a great idea to reverse engineer the goal and work backwards. To achieve 150 minutes of moderate intensity, you simply need 30 minutes a day, 5 days a week. Moderate activities include walking, jogging, swimming, and any recreational sport. You could also do 50-minute sessions, 3 days a week, depending on your schedule.

Another possible method is to go the route of high-intensity training, which includes sprinting, swimming, or joining a group fitness program. All it takes is just 75 minutes a week. That translates to 25-minute sessions, 3 days a week or 37-minute sessions just 2 days a week! Whichever route you choose to take, make sure to also include at least 2 days a week of strength training workouts that can last anywhere from 20-50 minutes. By doing so, you will increase lean muscle tissue, bone density, and metabolism.

Here is a working scenario for one of my clients. All names have been changed for privacy.

Sarah is a mother of 2, a high-performing manager with many obligations, and works on average 55 hours a week. Before training together, her schedule used to look like this:

6:30 a.m. — Wake up and make breakfast for herself and children

7:10 a.m. — Drop kids off at school and head to the office

8:00 a.m. — Work duties

12 p.m. — 50-minute lunch

5 p.m. — Work concludes

6-9 p.m. — Dinner and family time

9-10 p.m. — Time with spouse

With her schedule, we fit in working out at 5:45 a.m. She completes 30 minutes of strength and high-intensity training 2-3 days a week at the gym. On the remaining 2-3 days that week, she walks for 20 minutes during her lunch break and takes her dog for a quick 30-minute walk around the neighborhood with her family before dinner. She gets a solid 7 hours of sleep per night and starts her day energized, ready to take on whatever comes her way.

No matter how busy my clients are, if their goal is to get as healthy as they can, they are willing to make the time. They reschedule other events or go to bed an hour earlier in order to wake up earlier to get a workout in. Many people, me included, when starting out can fall susceptible to crazy powders, pills, and gadgets that promise magical weight loss and good health without doing anything. There is no such thing as "something for nothing," especially with our bodies. If we don't put in the time, energy, and commitment, our bodies cannot return high levels of energy, passion, creativity, and great health.

Health is something that we can all harness. I'll bet that if you're reading this, we are both nowhere near our full potential to what our life could be like. Imagine waking up energized every day and playing any recreational sport that you enjoy, pain-free. Many people tend to complain that exercise does not fit into their busy schedules. My clients have had many responsibilities, such as taking care of their children, parents, in-laws, or business, and are still able to find a few hours in their day to move their bodies. Everyone is busy, but that should inspire you to want to work out. A healthy body will help you to persevere through the busy days. Make your health a priority because without good health, you will not be able to enjoy the wealth of family and love.

CHAPTER 2

Why Health and Fitness are Vital

The US Centers for Disease Control and Prevention reported that over a quarter of the deaths from chronic diseases heart disease and stroke may have been prevented or prolonged by adopting a healthy lifestyle.*

The old saying that prevention is better than finding a cure could not be any more accurate. Not only will prevention save us from pain, it will also save us time and money. Medication and surgeries are not cheap, by any means. The extra hundred, thousand, or tens of thousands of dollars you spend could instead be invested into your health, preventing, or at the very least prolonging, the time needed before seeking medical assistance. Instead of spending time and money on different medications, spend time and money on taking care of the body through proper eating, exercise, and recovery habits.

Maintaining optimum health is important not only to us but also to our families, friends, and associates. When we are unhealthy, we place unnecessary stress and worry on our loved ones who end up suffering because of our choices. Since you are reading this, I hope that you are not the type of person who takes better care of your car than your own body. We would never purposely load the wrong fuel or liquid into our vehicles because doing so would cause the vehicle to malfunction. The same can be said with the human body. We should be mindful of what type of fuel we load into our bodies on a daily basis. Everyone wants to live a long and happy life for their spouse, children, and grandchildren, and for that reason alone I truly believe it is our responsibility to live and keep giving to those we love as long as we possibly can.

When was the last time you had an emergency that threw off your entire week or even months? I bet your own health and fitness was the last thing you were worried about, and that is okay! If you had settled for average health during that emergency, then your immune system most likely took a dive. A lower immune system can cause colds, weight gain, worsening blood markers, and fatigue. By striving for a higher level of fitness, we create a cushion for our health during these unexpected life events and emergencies. Many medical professionals agree that there are three major health levels: fit, normal, and sick.

*https://www.cdc.gov/healthreport/publications/compendium.pdf

Three Stages of Health

Fit—Fantastic blood markers, resting heart rate of 45-59 beats per minute. No problems running up a flight of stairs, and able to pick things up that weigh your body weight with ease.

Average—Average or slightly elevated blood markers, resting heart rate of 60-75 beats per minute. Running up a flight of stairs leaves you slightly winded and picking things up that weigh your body weight requires a great deal of effort.

Sick—Elevated blood markers, possibly on a few medications, resting heart rate of 80+ beats per minute, have difficulty walking up a flight of stairs and unable to pick things up that weight your body weight.

When life happens and the unexpected occurs, the fit person with high levels of energy and health will have a safety net should they stop exercising or eating properly for a period of time. They will instead have average health rather than excellent, a much better option than falling from average to sick health.

No matter where you are on that spectrum, it is always possible to build up your "health bank account." A great example is a client who was in the sick-to-average range. After months of working out and eating right, we brought her up to fit levels of health. Then, a major life crisis occurred, and she stopped working out and lost control of her eating for two months. However, because she had put in many months of work and built up her health bank account to fit levels, she only dropped to having average/slightly below average health. Imagine if she never made the commitment to get to the fit level and stayed in the sick-to-average range of health while this crisis occurred. Her health and blood markers could have become so poor that she would now have to pay hundreds of dollars per month for medications. Of course, that is a big hypothetical "what if" and anything is possible. However, I want to relay how vital it is to build up your health bank account for future emergencies that could occur at any point.

There is a saying that "health is the greatest wealth." I am not solely talking about monetary wealth, although that is a very important aspect. I am also talking about being wealthy in faith, love, passion, relationships, creativity, and high levels of energy. When I neglected certain parts of my life, I had less energy and passion to share with my family and loved ones. I thought it was because I was overworking myself, wearing many different hats and putting in an average of 65-90 hours a week. By improving what I ate, the way I worked out, incorporating a morning ritual (which we'll get into in a later chapter), and ensuring I wasn't skimping on my sleep, I felt like I could operate closer to my full capacity. Many studies recommend that even as adults we should strive to sleep at least 7-9 hours a night to perform our best the next day. Sleeping is massively underrated. For those thinking that we are "okay" with 4-6 hours of sleep, let me share with you that I have done the whole 4-6 hours of sleep. In fact, I would hold it like a badge of honor as you might do. I found that my enthusiasm, mental state, skills, and passion for life and my career were not at 100%. My mood was not the best, and I would get annoyed at the little things that never mattered to me before. I became dependent on heavy doses of caffeine. Depriving ourselves of sleep will hold us back from fully living our lives in business and with our family.

We owe it to ourselves and our loved ones to have the highest amount of energy, happiness, love and physical and spiritual wealth we can possibly achieve so that we can not only take care of ourselves but our loved ones as well. When flying, flight attendants will tell you to put your own mask on first and then help your child. Taking care of ourselves is not selfish but practical because it allows us to use our extra energy to fuel our work, relationships, and goals. I have had many people tell me that because of how busy they are with their family and children that they are unable to take care of their own health.

I believe that we should never use our family, kids or loved ones as an excuse to not take care of ourselves. Instead, use them as inspiration to improve your energy, health, passion, and overall quality of life. Without at least one strong emotional reason for wanting to change our health, we will never fully commit to the new lifestyle and persist, or push against resistance, when things get difficult.

One example would be a couple that I have worked with. They have five children and full-time jobs. No one forces them to exercise, consume a healthy diet, or practice persistence and self-love. They do all of the above because they know it would be unethical and irresponsible to their kids if they can't be there for them. Their children fuel their drives to massively reduce their risk from preventable diseases, such as Type 2 diabetes, hypertension, heart attacks, and strokes. They both made a commitment to adopt healthy eating habits and exercise for at least one hour 3-5 days a week.

Because of their change in habits, they lost over 80 pounds in a year. With newfound levels of energy and improved self-esteem, they can now show and teach their children, who will hopefully teach and inspire their children about making healthier choices. That is what we call Generational Health.

Health = Wealth

Over the course of training hundreds of people with diverse backgrounds, I noticed that many of my clients received a raise or promotion at work or found the courage to pursue their dream once they got their health and fitness in check. From my observation, nearly everyone who has incorporated proper nutrition and exercise also experiences some sort of personal progress. They start to walk differently, with their shoulders back, chest out, and a smile on their face. Their postural muscles in their shoulder and back are stronger so they are no longer slouching. They have built stronger forearms, which easily allow them to deliver a firm handshake. They have a stronger set of legs that allow them to walk with speed and confidence. They look and feel much happier and healthier wearing clothes that look great on them. On top of all of that, they also become mentally and emotionally fit. Overcoming many setbacks in your health journey builds persistence. Keeping your promises builds commitment. Achieving your goals builds confidence. Understand that nothing is a quick fix. It is about long term consistency.

Is this all a coincidence? I cannot scientifically prove that having a commitment to a greater level of health and fitness increases your chances of improving your career or passion. However, there are studies that show the correlation in companies that have a wellness program with lower sick leave and higher productivity of up to 47%! Think about what that would do for your career if you were that much more productive.

I believe that awareness of the calories we expend and put into our body require a similar mental discipline as understanding your finances. When we become aware of what foods work with our bodies, we also become aware of what gives us energy and what drains our energy.

When people experience significant change in their lives, they typically stop taking proper care of themselves and put their focus on that change. Now, I totally understand that a business and certain careers can easily consume 12+ hours a day. Remember that all we need to reap health benefits is just 45-minute workouts 2-4 days a week, which would consist of resistance training and cardiovascular work. We all have 168 hours a week and that if we sleep a typical 7 hours to feel recuperated, we would have 17 hours left in the day, and even if your career takes 12 hours a day, you would still have a solid **5 hours** for family, education, exercise, and leisure time. Make time and not excuses.

I had previously fallen into the trap of letting time control me rather than controlling time myself. An interesting paradox I have learned from a mentor is that the more structure, systems, and rules we put in place, the more freedom we obtain. In the past when I would complain about not having enough time, it was really just many wasted hours a week scrolling through social media or the news. I'll bet that if we audited your entire 168 hours in a week, we would discover that at least 10% of your time at work is spent on non-productive activities, such as scrolling on social media and texting. What if we completed our tasks sooner and did a better job because we were not distracted? We would have one less thing to stress about and enjoy higher satisfaction of being productive and adding value at our workplace.

Americans spend, on average, 4 hours a day watching the news, favorite shows, movies, and on social media. That is an average of 28 hours a week of downtime with which you just need to devote 3-7 hours a week for your health and longevity. This means that you can enjoy great health and also enjoy your favorite pastimes and shows with over 20 hours of leisure time per week.

It is never too late to get started on living a healthier life, as I've had many clients in their 50s, 60s, and even 70s make huge improvements in their everyday life. Some of these people were not even able to carry their own groceries, let alone their dream of holding their grandchildren. With just a few fundamentals, they are now able to carry their own groceries and pick up their grandchildren with ease. Depending on where you are in your fitness journey, it may take up to 6-18 months to fully transform your life. However, the time is going to pass anyway, so give your very best to improving your life.

CHAPTER 3

Massive Action

Action is the key player in the transformation of dreams from reality, and nonaction is a delusion that we will achieve something for nothing. Almost everything that occurs in our life is a result of our actions or inaction. Taking massive action now towards your health will ensure that you move towards your goals and create the momentum needed to break through the obstacles. It can be as easy as going for a 45-minute walk or eating a big bowl of colorful vegetables that you haven't eaten in a while. Our ancestors used to be very active, and for that reason, I highly recommend that we get some sort of physical activity every day. I am not suggesting that we all do brutal workouts every day, as that would be counterproductive to our health and longevity, unless you are an elite athlete with superb recovery protocols in place.

Here are a few ways that I like to have our clients take massive action from day one. What I am suggesting is that we get some sort of daily activity, whether it is playing with the kids, playing a recreational sport, walking your dog, and so on.

1. **Go for a power walk**. You immediately change your biochemistry by increasing blood flow, flooding your body with your natural morphine equivalent, endorphins. We are attempting to reprogram your mind and body to enjoy and become addicted to exercising to break old patterns. Your body will soon be craving the exercise and will experience another natural endorphin rush, putting you in a positive state of mind.

2. **Eat a big bowl of colorful vegetables**. By doing this, you are reinforcing your previous habit and commitment to your goals. In the early stages, every action that we can take and build positive reinforcement is a win, and that has been the foundation of our clients losing 50+ pounds and keeping it off.

3. **Tell 5 people closest to you about your commitment and have them all hold you accountable.** This is vital because there will be

days at the beginning of your journey where you will not feel motivated and possibly fall back into your old habits. There is a known three-week phenomenon where people lose motivation and quit altogether. Your inner circle of friends will be the key players in breaking past the first month. <u>Be sure to share your goals with people who you can trust and are committed to helping you become your best. When you surround yourself with people who support you, your success rate will dramatically improve</u>.

4. **Keep a journal.** Whether the journal is physical (offline) or digital (an online app), it is vital to be able to keep track of all of your progress from day one so that in times of difficulty you will be able to see how far you have come and use that to motivate you to continue your journey.

5. **Sign up for a class or trainer.** This step is recommended for people who don't trust themselves and feel the need for an expert to help them. By signing up for a class or with a trainer, you are showing commitment to a professional who will help you achieve your goals faster and in a safe manner. Even on the days you feel sluggish and unmotivated, as long as you

have a great coach, you will be able to push your body and get a great workout simply by showing up. I once tried to do my accounting on my own and probably spent over 100 hours trying to learn, read, and figure out what to do while running circles in my brain. Now my accountant will simply tell me what I need to do, saving me many hours of which I would then use to serve others in health and fitness. Always ensure that the trainer is a knowledgeable and reputable person who has experience helping people and has produced results of similar goals to yours.

6. **Work with an experienced friend or coach.** Before becoming a professional, I have experienced many injuries and did things without instructions to my knees, shoulders, and lower back from strength training because I simply searched on Google and assumed that I knew how to perform exercises correctly. It is important to perform all exercises correctly, but most importantly the mechanics of proper squatting, deadlifting, and pressing overhead because they have higher possibilities of injuries if done incorrectly over time.

Gratitude

Having an attitude of gratitude has tremendously improved my health, fitness, and overall wellness. Being grateful allows me to keep an open mind and create deeper connections.

I am so happy and grateful _____.

- I have all my physical limbs and senses.
- I get to wake up and do what I love.
- That the sun is out, and the birds are singing.
- For the warm cup of coffee I am enjoying.
- My parents are happy and healthy.
- My fiancée is loving, supportive, and patient.
- I have an unbelievable team that sincerely cares and wants the best for our fit fam.
- For our fit fam that allow us to be part of their journey.
- For the life-changing transformations and impact we continue to create in our community.
- To live a life of service and be able to provide value to others.

- For writing right now, for the positive impact this may make in your life.

Now that we have focused on what we are grateful for, let's move on to setting goals for the future.

Goals

A lack of clear, concrete goals is a huge contributor to why nearly 70% of Americans are overweight and obese. Most people never take the time to write down their goals. Many do not even know what their goal is until we ask them. The more specific your goal is, the higher the chance is that you will accomplish it. Instead of saying, "I just want to lose a few pounds and feel stronger," create a big goal with a strong reason about why it is important to you. Visualize a clear outcome for your goal with reasons to fuel your drive.

Here is how to change a simple goal to a more precise one:

"I will drop 50 pounds, have great blood markers in all areas and be able to deadlift my bodyweight and compete my first 5K running event. Dropping 50 pounds will take pressure off of my knees and will help reduce my risk of diabetes and heart disease, which will put my loved ones at ease and increase my quality of life with them."

Now visualize and let your body feel that experience. Our minds can't tell the difference between something real and something made up. When we imagine a scary or nerve-wracking moment, our heart starts to race, palms start sweating, and we take shallow breaths. Conversely, when imagining a beautiful moment, like your wedding day, holding your child for the first time, or traveling somewhere new, we remember how excited and happy that made us feel.

Doing this already puts your brain in a different thinking process, as you now know exactly what you want. Big spicy goals will excite, motivate, and inspire us to take action towards them. Also, at the moment of writing down your goal, you do not need to know how to accomplish that goal. Talk to an expert in the area of your goals or someone who has already achieved them, and they will help you figure out the "how" to achieve your goal.

As your health and fitness level improves so does your energy. This will allow you to take on new challenges. A quick tip is to word your goals as if you have already achieved them and create a vivid image in your mind of yourself achieving your goals. **Also, don't forget about who you need to become to achieve and attract your goals.** Visualize the person you wish to become to attract the good that you desire. Simple changes such as a certain posture, firm handshakes, smiling and loving more may have a tremendous impact in realizing your endeavors. It could also be major changes such as personality and attitude traits such as a pessimistic attitude that things are impossible, to an optimistic and positive attitude. Maybe we can become a more grateful, empathic, patience, caring, or candid individual.

Here are a few goals and affirmations, not limited to fitness, that I use as fuel to take action:

I am so happy and grateful for _____
_____,

- – I am creative, which allows me to stay ahead and continue to serve people in unique ways.
- – I am an effective, candid, and caring leader.
- – I am fit and healthy with great health markers.
- – I treat others with love and respect.
- – I am a student and lifelong learner.
- – Our team and I have empowered 1000 people to help 1000 people.

- Fighting Sickness with Fitness is known around the world.

Visualizing and having big dreams are fantastic, but unfortunately without mile markers along the way, we do not have a roadmap to achieve them. Short-term goals are great mile markers to achieve our long-term goals. For example, to practice being candid I will make it a goal to consistently provide constructive feedback to my team. For my health and fitness goal, I will have physical markers such as tracking my workouts from week to week, staying on top of my nutrition and also regularly getting my blood work done.

To be a lifelong learner, I will read a minimum of 30 minutes every day, keep an open mind and have mentors in my life.

I have always been a positive visionary, and I have visualized being a healthy and fit trainer running my own gym as a teenager way before I started exercising. I started the journey in my mind before taking consistent actions that allowed my dreams to become reality.

Responsibility

When I talk to my clients about changing their lives for the better and living a happier and healthier life, many would use their family as a reason for not taking care of themselves. We should never use our family as an excuse as to why we can't take care of ourselves. They should be one of the reasons why we would want to get healthy and reap the benefits of having great blood markers and higher energy levels. Taking full responsibility means that we will commit and make time for ourselves, have a plan of action and people that can help hold us accountable. We should all strive to operate at 100% of our capacity. Many people I have worked with have told me that they are now a better parent, grandparent, or spouse because they have higher levels of energy to keep up with their loved ones. Here are some responsible actions we can within the day to improve your health and energy tremendously.

1) Drink two cups of water now. Most of us are dehydrated, which tremendously decreases our mental and physical output.

2) Go for a 30-minute walk and get your blood flowing.

3) Have vegetables for your next meal.

4) Sleep 30 minutes earlier than you normally would.

Commitment

The degree of your commitment determines the results that you will attain. If you are 100% committed and have an attitude that you will achieve your goal no matter what, you will accomplish any goal. The people who have had the best results have always been the people who have had a massive desire and would not accept quitting even when challenges arose. As you go through your journey, your eating, sleeping, and exercise habits may cause you to completely change your schedule. When you are completely committed, you will gladly accept the changes because you know the long-term alternative is illnesses.

Structure = Freedom

With everyone busy with work, family, and other commitments, it is easy to forget to include yourself in the mix. When was the last time you were so worried about external circumstances that you didn't take care of yourself and were eating and drinking anything, anytime, or anywhere?

Consider a friend who has a regular job but barely makes it to work because he constantly snoozes the alarm and barely has enough time to get ready. With little time to prepare breakfast, he quickly heads down to the fast food store to grab a coffee with lots of sugar and a sandwich. A few hours later, he sits at work and complains about being tired, wanting to go home and rest. This person never gets his work done, and because of that, accumulates stress. The cycle continues and worsens until one day, the body can't take it anymore.

Let's compare this situation with a client who is a high-level executive. She wakes up before the early morning sun pours into the bedroom. She wakes before the alarm rings and preps for a morning workout. After exercising, she eats a well-balanced breakfast that she prepared the night before. She seems superhuman because of how much energy she has first thing in the morning and how she is able to maintain this energy throughout the rest of the day. The secret is having set rules to operate on to help structure the day.

It is highly tempting to have no structure and to just go about your day. The reason why many don't want structure in their lives is that they think it will somehow inhibit them from being free and cause them stress. This may sound contradictory but when you have structure in your life, you will notice how much free time you actually have. You will also feel less stressed because you have tackled the things that needed to be done. After many years of training clients, I noticed that those who have a mentality of exercising and eating whatever and whenever they want are less likely to achieve their goals and are more prone to creating unnecessary stress. Uncertainty is very stressful. Many CEOs and executives exercise before their workday and have some sort of structure and rules in place for their nutrition. Some claim to drink only black coffee and green tea in the morning, with maybe a piece of fruit, and eat a light lunch, such as a fish salad, so that they don't get weighed down and can maintain their energy.

Before you start thinking, "following rules is too rigid," remember that we follow rules every day at work. Back in my college days, when I had no rules for myself, I would party and stay up very late and pay for it in the morning by feeling sluggish. I lacked the motivation to do anything, let alone work out, and thereon wasted a day to recuperate.

Here are a few of my own rules that I follow. I am not suggesting that you do the same, but I want you to create a set of rules unique to yourself that will allow you to live a healthier and happier life.

- Get up at least 2 hours before my first appointment.
- Exercise every day first thing in the morning.

- Strength train at least 3 days a week.

- Drink at least 1 gallon of water every day.

- Consume at least 3 servings of fruits and veggies every day.

- Purchase organic and from local farmers when possible.

- Finish the most difficult task first thing in the morning.

- Read and educate myself at least 1 hour a day.

- Schedule time with family and loved ones.

- Schedule time for personal fulfillment.

CHAPTER 4

Eating for Health and Longevity

There are hundreds of different generic eating plans that will work on getting you to lose weight, but are they healthy and sustainable? Having been in this industry for nearly a decade, I have seen many fads and crazy diets promoted by some celebrities and actors. Here are some of the crazy eating habits that many of my clients have tried: Cabbage soup diet, 12 glasses of water and one slice of bread, no carbohydrates, including fruit, skipping meals and only eating one meal a day, liquid-only diet, and on and on. The reason why the above diets and other extreme diets fail is the expectation that the effects of the diet will last even without being on the diet anymore. Nearly everyone who starts one of those diets thinks they will only be adopting a new diet for a few months. Once they lose some weight, they go back to eating how they used to, not fully understanding that those magical effects only last while the diet lasts. I personally don't know anyone who can sustain a food group/type restriction diet for a year, let alone 5 to 10 years. Unfortunately, if we stop or go back to the type of eating that we did before, we will almost certainly gain all the weight back and possibly end up even heavier.

When we start speaking about longevity, one of the best ways to do so is to compare and follow similar eating habits of some of the healthiest and longest-living societies, such as the Mediterranean and Okinawan peoples. They have an average life expectancy that is much higher than traditional western societies, and this is what they have in common: They consume a wide variety of vegetables, fruits, nuts, whole grains, seeds, seafood, lean meats, and fatty fish.

Now that we know the foundation, here is where we will apply sports nutrition to increase exercise performance, which will, in turn, yield a higher return on our time and effort in the gym.

Step 1: Find daily caloric needs. A quick way to get an estimate is to use your current body weight and multiply it to get your daily calories.

Fat Loss: Multiply body weight by 11-13

<u>Maintenance</u>: Multiply body weight by 14-15

<u>Weight Gain</u>: Multiply body weight by 16-18

For example, if you weigh 180 pounds and want to lose weight, your total calories would be 180 x 12 which would be 2160 calories. Obviously, this quick and easy method does have its drawbacks because it doesn't take into account body composition and activity levels. I would suggest you stick with the calories that you get, but if you are losing weight too quickly, increase your daily calories by 200-300. If you are gaining weight too quickly, decrease calories by 200-300 daily.

Step 2: Finding macronutrient requirements. This part is very flexible and will vary greatly on trial and experimentation on yourself and seeing when you perform your best. I know some individuals who perform great on a higher-fat diet and some who thrive on a high-carb diet. The following are recommendations that are generally agreed on by professionals.

Carbohydrates: Contrary to popular belief, carbohydrates may make up a large portion of our daily overall calories. 35-65% of total calories should be coming from nutrient-dense carbohydrates such as leafy vegetables (spinach, kale, lettuce, etc.), root vegetables (sweet potato, yams, etc.), and fruits. The myth that still runs deep in the mind of people is that if you eat carbs at night, you will store fat. The fact is, eating too many calories above your maintenance needs will make you fat.

Protein: The daily intake of protein has always been controversial, with experts claiming low protein and others claiming high protein. The vast majority agree that having 15-35% of our total calories coming from protein is ideal and more than enough for health and strength building purposes. Protein sources should be varied throughout the week and may include the following but are not limited to organic, wild caught and cage-free eggs, salmon, tuna, chicken, beef, Greek yogurts, hemp, and soy, which all contain complete amino acid profiles necessary to repair and rebuild muscle from our workouts.

Fats: Since fats are essential for our brain, organs, and overall survival, it has been recommended that we consume 20-35% of our calories from fat. Healthy fat sources include avocados, nuts, seeds, and coconut and olive oils.

Step 3: Create an eating plan based on your lifestyle. After having hundreds of consultations, I completely understand that most of us will not be able to go home and cook all of our meals during the day. This is why I suggest that you plan ahead of time and create a menu. Just like achieving any other goal such as a business, family, or running a few errands, it is best to plan ahead and create a structure to accomplish these tasks in a time-efficient manner. Setting aside just one-two hours a week to prepare and cook your meals may be all it takes to get the results that you want.

Traditional Eating Plan

Below is a basic nutrition structure that works for many people due to its customizable design. Depending on your body type, activity level, and goals, vary the food portions accordingly. A great tool that I personally love to use and recommend is an app called **MyFitnessPal**, which makes tracking food much easier. Tracking your calories will teach you about the calories and macronutrients (protein, carbs, and fats) that are in our foods and will also show how many ounces/grams to consume. Similar to tracking our finances, we typically need to know what our budget is and keep tabs on how much we spend in order to not over consume, thereby falling into debt. Think of your daily calories as your budget. We can only do two things to ensure that we are on track to our goals, either eat your daily calories or increase your activity and metabolism. This does not mean that you will be tracking calories and macronutrients for the rest of your life. In a few months of doing this, you will understand your body enough where you will be able to provide the right foods for it out of habit. This also does not mean that you are manipulating your calories and filling up your calories with heavily processed and trans fats. Medical professionals agree that if we consume wholesome, unprocessed foods 80% of the time, most of our health problems would go away, while still allowing for some occasional "fun food." When possible, consume locally grown, grass-fed, organic and hormone-free products for the bulk of your food intake. I always try my best to have my clients choose and consume foods that they enjoy so that the process of getting healthy is much more enjoyable.

CARBOHYDRATES

Ezekiel bread

Whole wheat bread

Whole grain muffins

White rice

Brown rice

Quinoa

Whole wheat/grain Pasta

Black bean pasta

Beans (All)

Oatmeal

Oat flour

Coconut flour

Almond Flour

Whole wheat flour

VEGGIES

Broccoli

Green beans

Asparagus

Cucumber

Brussels sprouts

Spinach

Mushrooms

Cabbage

Cauliflower

Kale/Chard/Collard greens

Bell Peppers

Zucchini

Eggplant

Carrots

Tomatoes

Yellow onions

Sweet potatoes

Pumpkin

Acorn squash

Spaghetti squash

FRUITS

Bananas

Apples

Oranges

Berries (All)

Cherries

Grapefruit

Lemons/limes

Pineapples

PROTEINS

Eggs

Greek yogurt

Grass-fed beef

Hormone-free turkey

Hormone-free chicken

Wild caught salmon

Fresh tuna

FATS

Nuts (All)

Avocado

Guacamole

Almond butter

Peanut butter

Flax seed

Chia seeds

Hemp seeds

Sunflower seeds

Sesame seeds

Extra virgin olive oil

Coconut oil

Coconut butter

OTHERS

Stevia

Fresh herbs

Spices

Sriracha

Tabasco

Mustard

Salsa

Apple cider vinegar

Organic/Raw Honey

Pickles

Dark chocolate +70%

The Obesity Science studies have shown that meal frequency has minimal relevance in body composition and health benefits. This is because about 10-20% of calories are burned off per meal due to the thermic effect of food. For convenience, let's assume that we burn 10% of calories from the thermic effect of food. If you eat 6 small 300 calorie meals, you will burn 10% of it, which is 30 calories x 6 meals, burning off a total of 180 calories. When we eat 3 moderate 600 calorie meals, you will burn the same 10%, which is 60 calories x 3 meals, burning off the same 180 calories. This is why meal frequency makes almost no difference, as long as the total daily intake remains the same. I have used the 6 small meals to get in shape before, but for 90% of the population and for myself now, I highly recommend eating 1-4 bigger meals per day, which will leave you feeling more satisfied after each meal.

*Note—Any body composition change will almost always be a result of watching your daily caloric intake and having a balanced macronutrient and micronutrient intake.

With that being said, the following templates will have you eating 3 meals a day with 1 pre-workout snack, if you will be doing strength training or interval training that day.

The following plan is fantastic for anyone who is insulin-sensitive and over 20% body fat for men and 25% body fat for women.

Breakfast/Lunch

4-10 ounces protein

Unlimited leafy veggies of choice

1-2 servings healthy fats

Snack/Pre-workout

1-2 servings of fruits

Dinner

4-10 ounces of protein

Unlimited leafy veggies of choice

1-2 servings of healthy fats

1-2 servings of fruit

*Note—If you get in a solid meal 2-3 hours before your workout, your pre-workout meal may not be necessary but may help those with a faster metabolism and those who work out first thing in the morning and need to refill their glycogen stores to optimize their workout.

The following structure is fantastic for those who want to reap health benefits, get lean, and improve strength or high-intensity performance.

Breakfast/Lunch

4-10 ounces protein

Unlimited leafy veggies of choice

1-2 servings of healthy fats

Snack/Pre-workout

1-2 servings of fruits or 1-2 cups of starchy carbohydrate*

Dinner

4-10 ounces protein

Unlimited leafy veggies of choice

1-2 servings of healthy fats

1-4 servings of starchy carbohydrates*

*Starchy carbohydrates would be anything such as sweet potatoes, yams, oatmeal, rice, whole wheat bread, etc.

Free Meal/Cheat Meal Setup

This is an important topic to cover and learn about because having 1-2 "free meals" a week will help you stay consistent. No one can follow a nutrition program 100% of the time. Once you master this section of your program, I assure you that burning body fat, building muscle, or any other fitness goal will come more naturally. Based on my clients, the best times to have "free meals" are Friday evenings and/or Saturday/Sunday evenings.

Let's make this clear that this is not a license to binge on fast food and alcohol. The free meal is for you to enjoy a night out at a restaurant and not stress too much about what you can or cannot eat.

When possible, I recommend enjoying a higher carb meal with protein, such as sushi, pasta, and other rice meals. The thermic effect of food is much higher for carbs than fat, and in turn, we burn more calories just by eating! Also, with a higher carb meal, you will be storing the excess carbs in your muscles and liver as glycogen, which can store upwards of 400g (which is 2000 calories of carbohydrates).

Example of a Free Meal Day

Breakfast/Lunch

4-8 ounces any protein

Unlimited veggies

1-2 fruits of choice

Dinner

Pasta, sushi, or sandwich

Small dessert

Here is an example from one of my clients demonstrating a healthy lifestyle (name has been changed for privacy).

Jen is 350 pounds and a hardworking waitress. She typically picks up other people's shifts and ends up working an average of 12 hours a day with two 30-minute breaks in between. She wakes up at 6 a.m. to work out with a personal trainer, eats a healthy breakfast, and packs herself a dinner meal and snack for her 12-hour work shift. Since she works at a restaurant, her lunch is free. She decides on getting a fresh organic chicken salad with extra tomatoes and greens. At around 5 p.m., she gets a little hungry and takes her second break to eat her packed meal, which includes a fillet of salmon, mixed vegetables, and sliced up fruits to re-energize her for the rest of her shift. Once she gets home, she still has some calories left over, since she was eating high nutrient and low-calorie meals. She decides to finish off her evening with Greek yogurt and mixed berries.

This is just one example of how people who work 60+ hour weeks are able to make exercise and eating right a part of their lifestyle so long as they are willing to commit and plan ahead. Before moving on, I want you to commit to a schedule of working out and start making small changes in your dietary habits today.

CHAPTER 5

Fundamental Exercises

Out of the hundreds of exercises and variations, I want to share the tried and true exercises. These fundamental movements will carry you into more advanced exercises such as the Olympic lifts, the snatch, and clean and jerk. We simplified the exercise list based on human movements such as squatting, hip hinge to pick things up, pushing, pulling, and core.

Exercises

Jumping Jacks

- Variation 1: While standing up straight, simultaneously lift both arms to the side and above the head while your right foot steps out. Then bring both arms down to your side while stepping back in. Repeat with your left foot.

  - Good for those with knee issues

- Variation 2: Instead of stepping out one foot at a time, hop and separate your feet out while bringing your hands up. Then hop and bring your feet back together while you bring your hands back down.
  - More cardio

Arm circles

- Forward: arms straight out to the side, shoulder height, with palms facing up. Make circles with your arms starting your motion going forward. Start off with small circles and gradually get bigger.
- Backward: Same as forward but starting your motion going back.

Jog in Place

- Variation 1: light jog in one spot
- Variation 2: stand up with legs spread wider than shoulder width, slight squat, back straight and upright, move feet up and down as fast as you can landing on the balls of your feet ("Football run")
  - More cardio and speed

Burpee

Start in the standing position. Descend into a squat and place your hands on the ground shoulder width apart in front of you. Extend and kick back your legs into a plank/push-up position. Then, jump or step back into the previous squat position with your hands on the ground and stand up.

High knees

- While standing upright, bring one knee up in front of you as high as you can, lower, repeat on the other leg

  - Slower is good for stretching and for anyone with knee issues

  - Faster for more cardio

Alternating front kicks

- Standing upright, while raise one straight leg up while reaching to your toe with the opposite hand then bring back down. Repeat with the other leg. For example, if you kick your right leg up, you'd try to reach that leg's toes with your left hand, bring the leg back down. Then repeat with your left leg and right hand.

- o Tips: don't kick too high to prevent falling on your back; walk forward as you alternate your kicks

Butt kicks

- Standing upright, bend one leg at the knee and try to touch your heel to your butt (if you can't reach yet, that's okay. Just go as far as you can), lower back to starting. Repeat on the other leg.
  - o Slower is good for stretching and for anyone with knee issues
  - o Faster for more cardio

Push-up

- For beginner variations, simply change the starting position. Start on your knees instead. Remember to keep the hips forward while performing the push-up.

- Push-up against the wall: Hands out in front on the wall, shoulder height and slightly wider apart. Take a few steps back so that your body is at a slight diagonal. Keep your elbows close to your body and not flared out. Be aware that you don't bonk your head on the wall.

- For intermediate variations change the starting position to performing push-ups on your knees or toes.

Plyo push-up

- No matter which variation (wall, knees, or standard), a plyo push-up is adding a new element to it, a slight hop with your hands. As you push yourself up, you're pushing with enough force to get your hands off the wall or ground. Be careful that you're ready for this exercise and will avoid hitting the wall or ground with your face.

Narrow stance push-up

- Similar to a push-up (whether on the wall, knees, or standard), except your hands are slightly further in so the space between your hands are smaller. Remember to keep your elbows close to your body and not flared out. This exercise will engage your triceps more.

Wide stance push-up

- Similar to a push-up (wall, knees, or standard), except your hands are further apart. Keep your elbows from flaring outward. This will engage more of your shoulders and upper back.

Bodyweight Squat

Start by standing at shoulder's width apart with your toes slightly turned out. Sit your hips back and descend as if you were sitting on a chair. Once your hips become parallel with your knees, engage your glutes and begin to stand.

Squat jump

- Variation 1: Similar to a regular squat, except when coming back up, reach to the sky with your arms and stand on your tippy toes.

  o Better for people where impact is hard on their knees

- Variation 2: Similar to a regular squat, except you're trying to explode off the ground when coming back up. Land with "soft knees" as in land on the balls of your feet instead of stomping. Use your arms to help propel you up and keep balance.

Mountain climber

- Similar to a push-up, hands and wrists in line/ underneath the shoulder, arms straight

- Variation 1: Bring up one knee at a time, driving to your chest.

- Variation 2: Quicken your pace
- Variation 3: If available, use sliders underneath your feet for less friction and more speed
- Modification: Instead of in a plank position on the ground, plank on a higher surface like a table or bench. Make sure your body is at a diagonal with the ground.

Alternating mountain climber

- Instead of driving your knee only to your chest, drive it to the opposite side elbow. For example, you would drive your right knee to your left elbow, come back to starting, then your left knee to your right elbow.
- Mod: Do with hands or forearms on a surface like a table or bench, less body weight to hold up

Outside mountain climber

- Instead of driving your knee to your chest, take one foot and bring it as far up to the outside of your hand. Bring it back to starting and repeat with the other foot.
  - Pick up the pace for more cardio and difficulty.

      o   Mod: Do with hands or forearms on a surface like a table or bench, less body weight to hold up

Plank

- Come down on your elbows with your legs stretched out behind you and toes pointed down. Hold your hips and spine in a neutral position while contracting the abdominals.

Hands to Elbow

- Start in a push-up position with the hands shoulder width apart. Brace your core and slowly descend from your hands and down to your elbows in a plank position and then slowly back up on your hands.

Side plank

- Variation 1: Lie on your side with your feet connected and with your arm directly under your shoulder. Elevate hips to maintain a neutral spine from head to toe and contract.

Grass picker

- Variation 1: Step out to one side so that your feet are wider than shoulder-width. Perform a bodyweight squat and pretend you're "picking grass" or scooping with the same side arm you stepped out with, then stand back up to starting and repeat with the other side. For example, if you stepped out with your right leg, you'd "scoop" with your right arm.

- Variation 2: Hop your legs out to wider than shoulder-width, perform a bodyweight squat and "pick grass" with one arm, then hop back to starting. Repeat and "pick grass" with the other arm this time.

- Tips for both: when squatting, watch that your toes don't go past your knees. If it does, you'll need to adjust so that your butt is pushed back more when squatting or widen your stance. To get the full motion, make sure you're not just lifting your butt in the air and straightening your knees so you're close enough to the ground to "pick grass."

Cross jacks

- Variation 1: Step out with your right foot (like a jumping jack) and bring both arms out to your side at shoulder height. When stepping back in, your right foot will cross in front of your left foot and your right arm will be crossed on top of your left arm. Go back to starting position. Repeat, but this time step out with your left foot with arms at shoulder height. Then cross your left foot in front of your right and your left arm will be crossed on top of your right. Repeat alternating which arm and leg will be on top/in front.

- ○ Better for people with knee issues

- Variation 2: Same as variation 1 but hopping out with both feet and hopping in with one crossed in front of the other.

- ○ More cardio

Skiers

- Starting at standing position with feet shoulder-width apart, bend over so that your knees are slightly bent, you're hinged at the hips with your butt pushed back, and your back is almost parallel to the ground.

- ○ Variation 1: Take a wide sidestep to the right, then tap your left foot on the ground crossing behind your right foot. Then take a wide sidestep to the left, tapping your right foot after it crosses behind your left foot. Make sure to stay hinged at your hips and back almost parallel to the ground.

- This variation is good for those whose knees are affected by impact.

○ Variation 2: Similar to variation 1, except you're hopping from side to side instead of stepping. If it feels more comfortable, you can leave your foot that gets crossed behind off the ground. It doesn't have to tap the ground unless you need it to keep your balance.

- This variation will bring your heart rate up faster, more cardio.

○ Variation 3: Add a hip circle resistance band right above your knees for an extra challenge.

Superman

Lie flat on your stomach with your hands out in front of you and slowly extend your spine by raising your upper body and legs up simultaneously. If you have shoulder problems, I would recommend that you place your arms beside your hip while performing the movement.

Lunge

- Lunges are a great exercise that nearly anyone can do and require no equipment, although depending on your fitness level you could also use weights. Keep a proud, upright posture and engage the core as you take a big step forward. Bend at the knees and pause a few inches off of the ground. A common issue for many people is leaning too far forward, with their knees passing the toes. This strains the knees unnecessarily and can cause injury. Your bent knee should not extend past your toes.

Walking lunge

- Similar to regular lunges, but instead of coming back to center after each lunge, you continue to lunge forward, alternating the leg you step forward with. You'll end up going a certain distance, whether that's the length your office building, backyard, or the length of the basketball court in your neighborhood.

Reverse lunge

- Similar to regular lunges, but instead of stepping forward, step backwards. Your front leg should form about a 90-degree angle and your back knee should be a few inches off the ground. Come back to center and alternate which leg you step back with. Make sure your body is upright and not hunched over. Keep in mind that your knee should not pass your toes.

Lateral lunge

- Instead of stepping forward or backwards, step out to the side with your hips still facing forward. Just like regular lunges, watch that your knee doesn't go past your toes. As you come down in a lateral lunge, the side that you're lunging, shoot that hip back like you're coming down to sit in a chair. You should feel a stretch in your opposite leg's hamstring (the backside to your thigh). Come back to center and lunge to the other side.

Blackburn

- Starting with laying on your stomach. Your feet will stay on the ground for this exercise. Start with your arms out in front above your head, parallel to the ground with your palms facing down. As you bring your arms around to your side, slowly rotate your hands so that your palms are facing up, bend your arms, and rest your hands on the small of your back, one on top of the other. Bring your elbows together and squeeze your shoulder blades. Avoid stretching out your arms when you squeeze your shoulder blades. Your hands should still be on the small of your back and elbows bent. After you've squeezed your shoulder blades together for one or two seconds, release and bring your arms out to the side again and slowly rotate your palms to face the ground as your arms and hands come back to above your head, your starting position.

- o Good prehab exercise to strengthen the rotator cuff to help prevent injuries.

Kettlebell lunge

- Variation 1: Same movements as a regular lunge but holding a kettlebell close to your chest. Keep your elbows tucked, instead of flaring out. Make sure the kettlebell is close to your body to help avoid unnecessary injury to your shoulders.

- Variation 2: Same movements as a regular lunge, but holding two kettlebells, one in each hand. The kettlebells will be next to the sides of your body, just hanging. Keep arms and kettlebells at your side while you alternate your lunges.

Kettlebell Deadlift

- Place the kettlebell between your feet. Hinge and bend at the hips while keeping a neutral spine and tension in your hamstrings and glutes. Once you grab ahold of the kettlebell, brace your abdominals, hamstrings, and glutes and extend/ stand upright by pushing your glutes forward. Hinge again at the hips while maintaining full contraction until the kettlebell is back on the ground.

Kettlebell Swing

- Start by standing shoulder width apart and place the kettlebell about a foot away. Before grabbing it and swinging it incorrectly, practice hinging at the hips and bracing the core while hiking the kettlebell into your hips. Use the momentum to put the kettlebell back in starting position. Once this phase can be completed with one motion, move to the next step.

- Once you hike the kettlebell into your hips, you want to immediately pop and snap at your hips forward. While keeping your core, lats, and lower body contracted, allow gravity to pull the kettlebell back down to your hips and repeat.

Kettlebell single arm swing

- Stance is the same as a regular Kettlebell Swing. However, you'll be holding the kettlebell with just one hand. Do half the reps with your right hand holding the weight, then the other half of the reps with your left hand. Still remember to pop your hips and squeeze your butt when your hips are popped forward. In addition, don't muscle up the weight. Use the power from your hips to bring the weight up.

Kettlebell squat

- Variation 1: Kettlebell box squat—Squat down like you're sitting in a chair until your bottom actually reaches the box or bench, then stand back up. Be aware that the box or bench you use isn't too high that when you sit, your feet are off the ground. Your feet should still be able to be flat on the ground when sitting on the box or bench.

Kettlebell single arm lunge

- Variation 1: Only the hand opposite of the leg stepping forward to do the lunge will hold the kettlebell. For example, if you're stepping forward to lunge with your left foot, your right hand will be holding the weight. Similarly, if you're stepping forward with your right foot, your left hand will be holding the kettlebell. Complete half of the reps on one side before switching to the other. Be mindful that your knee is not passing your toes when you're lunging and that your body is upright and not hunched over.

Kettlebell single arm deadlift

- Only one hand is holding a kettlebell. The leg that's going back in the air will be the side your kettlebell is on. For example, your left leg is your planted leg. It has a slight bend, not locked. Your right hand has the kettlebell. As you balance on your left leg and your right arm is coming down to the ground, your right leg will be straight and going behind you. Keep your shoulders back. Avoid a rounded back as you bring the kettlebell down. Do half the reps all on one side before switching legs.

  - If you need extra support for balance, stand about an arm's distance away from a wall and put just your fingertips on the wall for support as needed.

Single arm kettlebell squat

- Instead of holding the kettlebell with two hands, only one hand will be supporting the weight. Grip the handle with your hand but flip the kettlebell so that the bottom part is resting on your wrist. Don't collapse your wrist; keep it straight and sturdy. Just like a regular kettlebell squat, keep your elbow tucked and not flared out. Do half of the reps on one side and half the reps on the other side.

Dumbbell Curl to Press

- Stand at shoulder width apart and have your palms facing forward. Keep your elbows tight and curl the dumbbells all the way up to your shoulders by using your biceps. Twist your wrists so that your palms are pointing forward again and push straight up over your head. A quick key to knowing if you are performing this correctly is if your elbows are in line with your ears as you are pushing the dumbbells overhead.

Dumbbell front to lateral raise

- Grab a lighter than usual set of dumbbells. We want to go a bit lighter since the dumbbells will be farther away from our body, thus adding more strain to our shoulders.

- Variation 1: Start with arms straight and palms facing the front of your thighs. Bring your arms in front of your body to shoulder height, then bring the dumbbells back down to your thighs. Shift so that your palms are now facing the sides of your thighs. Bring your straight arms up to shoulder height, then back down. All of those movements together make one rep.

- Variation 2: Start with arms straight and palms facing the front of your thighs. Bring your arms in front of your body to shoulder height, then rotate so that your arms are still shoulder height, but off to the side.

Single Hand dumbbell row

- For this variation, you'll need something like a high box or bench to use for support. Your feet are staggered with the side that is holding the dumbbell in back. Your front leg is slightly bent. You're bent at your hips with your butt pushed back and your back almost parallel to the ground. One arm is used as a brace, while the other is holding the dumbbell. Bring the dumbbell to about your armpit. Don't flare your elbow out, keep it close to your body. After doing half the reps, switch your stance and the side the dumbbell is on. Complete other half of reps.

Dumbbell Row

- Bend 45 degrees at the hips while bracing your core and maintaining a neutral spine, then pull the dumbbells towards your hips driving your elbows behind your body while squeezing your shoulder blades together.

Ab Kickout

- Comfortably sit and place your hands shoulder width apart and slightly lean back. Lean into your hands, lifting your feet off the ground. Engage your core and bring your knees to your chest and then extend your legs then repeat.

Lying Leg Raise

- Lie flat on your back with your hands under your hips for support. Engage your core and start to elevate your legs all the way up. Then, slowly lower your legs until they are an inch or two off the ground.

Butterfly crunch

- Lay on your back with your legs forming a 90-degree angle. Begin with your arms above your head, then as your swoop your arms to your side, crunch up and try to touch your fingertips behind your legs. Try to get your shoulder blades as high off the ground as you can. Come back down as you bring your hands to starting position above your head. Your legs stay in the 90-degree position the whole time. Some things to remember is that to avoid neck injury, be mindful that you're not tucking your chin nor trying to look back. As you crunch up, look up at the sky.

- Modification: reach to the outsides of your thighs instead of behind your legs.

Russian Twist

- Variation 1: Sit on your bottom with your knees up and feet flat on the ground. Lean back far enough so that you can feel your core contract to hold you up, but not too far back that you'll fall over. Twist your torso to the right until both of your hands touch the ground. Twist to the left. Be conscientious, especially as you start to feel tired and your core starts to burn, that you're still leaned back so you're using your core.

- Variation 2: Same movements as variation 1, except your feet are hovering above the ground. You'll need to have a stronger core for this movement to keep your balance. Twist your torso right and left like in variation 1 while trying to touch the ground with both hands on each side.

- Variation 3: Same movements as variation 2, except add a weight to touch the ground as you twist instead of just touching the ground with your hands

Bench dip

- This can be done on a chair, bed, bench, or anything sturdy that's about comfortable sitting height. This exercise targets your triceps.

- Variation 1: Start by sitting on the edge of the bench with your feet on the ground. Place your hands right next to your thighs, palms on the bench, fingertips over the edge. Walk your feet out so that your back is still fairly close to the bench and your legs form a 90-degree angle. Lower yourself so that your arms form about a 90-degree angle. Push yourself back up while leaving your legs and feet at a 90-degree angle.

- Variation 2: Similar to variation 1, except instead of your legs forming a 90-degree angle, your legs are straight and you're balancing on your heels. Dip so that your arms form a 90-degree angle and come back up to complete a rep.

- Variation 3: To add more depth to your dip, place a box under your feet to add elevation to your straight legs. Perform a dip.

Hip Bridge

- Start by lying flat on your back with your knees bent and about a foot away from your glutes. Extend your hips up and push through your heels until you reach full extension, then slowly descend down.

Box step-up

- Use a sturdy wooden or hard plastic box to step on. Face the box. Step up one foot at a time. If you need the extra support, lightly push on the knee of the first leg you use to step up. Step down one foot at a time. Alternate what leg you use to step up first with. As you get stronger, use a higher box, quicken your pace, and/or add dumbbells to hold with your hands.

Lateral box step-up

- Use a sturdy wooden or hard plastic box to step on. Instead of facing the box, stand to the side of it. Sidestep up with your inside leg. Follow with your other leg. Step down on the other side, one leg at a time. For example, if you're standing on the left side of the box, you'd sidestep up with your right leg and follow with your left leg. Then sidestep down with your right leg followed by your left leg to be set before then sidestepping up with your left leg now and following with your right leg.

- As you quicken your pace and keep balance, you don't need to have both feet set on the ground before alternating to the other leg. For example, after you sidestep up with your right foot, then sidestep down with your right foot, you don't need to bring your left foot all the way down. You can leave it on the box and push off from there.

Alternating shoulder press

- Like a military press, but instead of pressing both dumbbells up at the same time, only press one arm up at a time. Still keep in mind that when you press up, your elbows should be by your ear to help prevent unnecessary shoulder strain.

Kettlebell squat to shoulder press

- There are two ways you can hold the kettlebell: by the handles or flipped upside down and cupped like a goblet. Either way, keep the kettlebell close to your body as well as your elbows tucked close to your body, not flared out. While holding the kettlebell near your chest, perform a regular

Kettlebell squat. Stay upright, shoot that booty back, and watch that your knees don't pass your toes. Squat down, then come back to starting, then press the kettlebell above your head making sure that your elbows are by your ears. Bring the kettlebell straight back down to starting position. That's one rep.

Tabata

- An interval-timed type of workout that is high-intensity with a short exercise time and short rest. A Tabata is a total of eight rounds, 20 seconds on and 10 seconds off. If there are two exercises listed for Tabata, perform each exercise four times, alternating between the two.

Back extension

- Variation: Maintain a neutral spine from head to lower back. Adjust the seat so that your hip crease is across the top of the pad allowing you to bend at the waist. Start bending forward slowly at the waist until you can no longer maintain a neutral spine. Slowly rise back up until neutral spine is maintained.

- Variation: Weighted back extension

Lateral raise

- Grab a set of dumbbells that are a little lighter than you would normally use. Since this exercise requires that the weight is farther away from the body, it can cause more stress on the shoulders. To help prevent injuries, we recommend that you go a bit lighter than usual. Test out the weight and adjust as needed. When you have a set picked out and in your hands, stand up straight with a slight bend in your knees, face your palms towards the side of your thighs, arms straight. Raise your arms straight up to shoulder height. Your legs and arms should be forming a capital T. Nice and controlled, bring your arms back to starting.

Reverse flies

- Similar to lateral raises, don't grab a weight that's too heavy or it will cause shoulder strain. Keep your feet shoulder-width apart, knees slightly bent. Bend at your hips so that your butt is sticking out and your back is almost parallel to the ground. Your arms with the weights start by hanging straight down, then as you squeeze your shoulder blades together, lift the weights laterally to shoulder height. Keep a slight bend in your elbows. Stay in control of the weight as you lower it back to starting position.

Bulgarian split squats

- This exercise will really work your booty and balance. However, if you have knee issues, it would be better to do this exercise on a lower platform.

- Have a low stool, bench, or box behind you. Take a step away from the bench. With one foot planted on the ground, lift your other leg behind you so that the top of your foot or toes are on the bench for support. While balancing on your planted foot, squat so that your planted leg forms about a 90-degree angle. Your back leg will bend as well. Keep your body upright when you perform the split squat. Watch that your knee doesn't pass your toes when you squat down. If it does, carefully hop or wiggle your planted foot further from the bench. Do half the reps on one side, then switch.

- To add more difficulty, hold a dumbbell in each hand or position a barbell for a back squat. Add more or less weight as needed.

Band pull apart

- Use a long resistance band of appropriate thickness. Grip the band at its ends either overhand or underhand. Keep tension on the band. It shouldn't look like a limp noodle. Hold the band out in front, chest height. Keeping your arms straight, pull the band apart to your chest and squeeze your shoulder blades together with control, then come back to starting. YOU are in control of the band the whole time. Don't let it snap you back. If it's not challenging enough, walk your hands closer together, then perform the band pull apart. The further your hands are in and closer together they are, the harder it will be to pull apart. Similarly, if it's a bit too challenging, walk your hands further away from each other. If you're gripping the ends already and it's still a bit too challenging, loop just your thumbs through instead of gripping the band with your whole hand. If it's still too challenging, grab a band that's thinner and has less tension.

Farmer's walk

- Imagine farmers carrying buckets on each side of them day in and day out. You'll be like that, except with dumbbells or kettlebells. Grip the weight so that you're working your forearms. Keep in mind that you want to be walking with your shoulders back and great posture. Contract your core while you walk the specified distance.

Overhead Farmer's Walk

- You can use any type of weight (set of dumbbells, set of kettlebells, medicine ball, a bumper plate). Hold the weight straight up above your head with both hands. If you have a set of dumbbells or kettlebells, you'll have one in each hand. For kettlebells, you'll hold it by the handles, and the weight will rest of the outside of your straight wrist. Make sure that with whatever weight you choose to use, you keep your arms close to your ears. Having the weight too far forward or backwards will cause unnecessary shoulder strain. Keeping your core tight and the weight straight up above your head, walk the specified distance.

Weighted plank hold

- Similar to a regular plank, except a bumper plate weight or chain is on your back or you have on a weighted vest.

Military press

- Start by standing or sitting up straight with great posture while holding the dumbbells by your shoulders. Keep your palms facing forward, your wrists straight, and elbows out to form about 90-degree angles. Push the dumbbells straight up towards the sky keeping your elbows and arms in line with your ears. If your arms are too far forward or back, it'll put too much strain on your shoulders and you'll be more prone to injury, especially as the weights get heavier. With control, lower the dumbbells back to the starting position.

Cuban press

- Standing straight with a set of lighter dumbbells in your hands, face your palms towards your thighs, shoulders back and arms straight. Bring the dumbbells up, almost like you're dragging them along your body. Your elbows will be pointed out to the side instead of pointed backward. Once you reach chest height, rotate your shoulder and the dumbbells so that you're in a Military Press position. Like a Military Press, press up above your head and keep it controlled back down to your shoulder. Rotate and flip the weights back down so that your palms are facing your body again and your elbows are pointed out to the side. With control and dumbbells close to your body, lower back to starting position.

Triceps band pushdowns

- Standing upright with a slight bend forward at the hips, grab the band with your palms facing in. Focus on extending your elbow down until fully locked out while keeping the shoulders locked in. Control the band back up and maintain tension on the band.

General Strength and Fitness Workouts

The following are workouts that require the bare bones fitness equipment and a simple pair of dumbbells and kettlebells, bands, and some suspension trainers. These workouts are beneficial for all levels of fitness and fantastic for beginner and intermediate trainees if your goal is to get healthy by building foundational strength, increasing your cardiovascular system, and increasing your metabolism to help you burn body fat.

Warm up

I highly recommend that you perform at least five minutes of a dynamic workout that will elevate your heart rate, prime the nervous system, and stretch the muscles through its range of motion.

Example dynamic workout

Jumping jacks x 45 seconds

High knees x 45 seconds

Butt kicks x 45 seconds

Squat x 45 seconds

Push-ups x 45 seconds

Arm circles x 45 seconds

200m jog

If you still have stiff or tight muscles after the warm-up, I highly recommend incorporating a quick five-minute mobility and self-myofascial release work using foam rollers and lacrosse balls in your tight areas. Please call our gym or reach out to www.YanagidaFitness.com for more in-depth detail.

*Note: **Stay Hydrated!** Being hydrated before, during, and after a workout is crucial for health but particularly important during exercise. Just 2% of dehydration of the body can cause dizziness, muscle cramps, and nausea during a workout. Studies suggest drinking 16-32 ounces of water 2-3 hours before a workout and 8-16 ounces of water every 30 minutes during your workout.

Workout #1

Squat

Push Up

Mountain Climber

Plank

Perform each exercise for 40 seconds and rest for 20 seconds before moving on to the next exercise. After all four exercises have been completed, take a quick 30-90 second recovery. Depending on your fitness level, repeat another 1-4 rounds.

Workout #2

Cross Jacks

Grass Picker

Skiers

Superman

Perform each exercise for 40 seconds and then rest for 20 seconds before moving on to the next exercise. After all four exercises have been completed, take a quick 30-90 second recovery. Depending on your fitness level, repeat another 1-4 rounds.

Workout #3

Lunges

Narrow Stance Push Up

High Knees

Burpees

Perform each exercise for 40 seconds and then rest for 20 seconds before moving on to the next exercise. After all four exercises have been completed, take a quick 30-90 second recovery. Depending on your fitness level, repeat another 1-4 rounds.

Workout #4

High Knees

Leg Raises

Plank

Mountain Climber

Perform each exercise for 40 seconds and then rest for 20 seconds before moving on to the next exercise. After all four exercises have been completed, take a quick 30-90 second recovery. Depending on your fitness level, repeat another 1-4 rounds.

Workout #5

Kettlebell Swing
Dumbbell Curl to Shoulder Press
Kettlebell Squat
Flutter Kicks

Perform each exercise for 40 seconds and then rest for 20 seconds before moving on to the next exercise. After all four exercises have been completed, take a quick 30-90 second recovery. Depending on your fitness level, repeat another 1-4 rounds.

Workout #6

Kettlebell Lunge
Dumbbell Row
Burpee
Ab Kickouts

Perform each exercise for 40 seconds and then rest for 20 seconds before moving on to the next exercise. After all four exercises have been completed, take a quick 30-90 second recovery. Depending on your fitness level, repeat another 1-4 rounds.

Workout #7

Kettlebell Squat
Bench Dip
Dumbbell Row
Hip Bridges

Perform each exercise for 40 seconds and then rest for 20 seconds before moving on to the next exercise. After all four of the exercises have been completed, take a quick 30-90 second recovery. Depending on your fitness level, repeat another 1-4 rounds.

Workout #8

Kettlebell Lunge
Narrow Push Up
Band Pull Apart
Hands to Elbow Plank

Perform each exercise for 40 seconds and then rest for 20 seconds before moving on to the next exercise. After all four exercises have been completed, take a quick 30-90 second recovery. Depending on your fitness level, repeat another 1-4 rounds.

Workout #9

Kettlebell Squat
Kettlebell Swing
Kettlebell Deadlift
Plank

Perform each exercise for 40 seconds and then rest for 20 seconds before moving on to the next exercise. After all four exercises have been completed, take a quick 30-90 second recovery. Depending on your fitness level, repeat another 1-4 rounds.

Workout #10

Military Press
Dumbbell Row
Kettlebell Swing
Push-Up

Perform each exercise for 40 seconds and then rest for 20 seconds before moving on to the next exercise. After all four exercises have been completed, take a quick 30-90 second recovery. Depending on your fitness level, repeat another 1-4 rounds.

CHAPTER 6

The Power of Tabata

The Tabata Training Protocol founded by Dr. Izumi Tabata is one of the most time-efficient workouts that we can do to increase aerobic and anaerobic fitness. It can be done in just 4 minutes! Dr. Tabata took two groups of high-level athletes through six weeks of training, one group doing 60 minutes of aerobic training at 70% and the other group performing sprints using his protocol of 20-second sprints followed by 10 seconds of rest repeated 8 rounds for a total of 4 minutes.

The aerobic training group increased their aerobic capacity by 9.5% and anaerobic capacity by 0%.

The Tabata training group increased their aerobic capacity by **14%** and anaerobic capacity by **28%.**

Another great benefit that you will reap is that due to its intense workout nature, the Tabata training protocol will elevate your metabolism from the Excess Post

Oxygen Consumption (EPOC) and will keep it high for many hours after the workout itself. That is one of the many great reasons why many trainers and coaches will use this protocol to help clients get healthy and lean in the shortest amount of time safely.

Before giving 100% maximal effort into the Tabata protocol, go through a five-ten minute warm up to get your body ready for the workout.

I must warn that this is an intense training protocol. I would recommend that you have at least a minimum of three-six months of working out under your belt, have proper exercise mechanics, and have both your nutrition and hydration in place. This program can result in great benefits but will leave you winded no matter how athletic you are.

Tabata #1
Sprint

For 20 seconds, sprint at 100% maximal effort followed by a brief 10 seconds of rest. Repeat the sprints for 8 total rounds for a complete 4 minutes. You'll soon understand why.

*Note: If this is your first time as a beginner, double the rest period for a total of 20 seconds for a few weeks and once you acclimate, perform the original protocol.

Tabata #2
Stationary Cycling

For 20 seconds, cycle and pedal at 100% maximal effort followed by a brief 10 seconds of rest. Repeat for 8 total rounds for a complete 4 minutes.

*Note: If this is your first time as a beginner, double the rest period for a total of 20 seconds for a few weeks and once you acclimate, go back to the original protocol.

Tabata #3
Rowing Machine

For 20 seconds, row at 100% maximal effort followed by a brief 10 seconds of rest. Repeat for 8 total rounds for a complete 4 minutes.

*Note: If this is your first time as a beginner, double the rest period for a total of 20 seconds for a few weeks and once you acclimate, go back to the original protocol.

Tabata #4
Jumping Rope

This one may be a bit difficult if you are quite new to jumping rope. If the last time you jumped rope was 10 years ago, I would recommend practicing jumping rope and then using the Tabata protocol so that you can generate maximal force.

For 20 seconds, jump rope at 100% maximal effort followed by a brief 10 seconds of rest. Repeat this for 8 total rounds for a complete 4 minutes.

Modified Tabata

If you feel that a true Tabata training protocol of doing solely one exercise and muscle group is too intense for you, here is the modified series of Tabata that also works fantastic, giving great benefits in a short amount of time.

Tabata #5
Burpee

Mountain Climber

Train and push your body to perform each exercise for 20 seconds at 100% effort followed by a brief 10 seconds of rest. Perform exercises back to back in a circuit fashion and perform the following exercises for 4 total rounds. Once you complete 4 rounds (4 minutes), take a 60-90 second break and then decide if you would like to perform an additional round.

Tabata #6
Grass Picker
High Knees

Train and push your body to perform each exercise for 20 seconds at 100% effort followed by a brief 10 seconds of rest. Perform exercises back-to-back in a circuit fashion and perform the following exercises for 4 total rounds. Once you complete 4 rounds (4 minutes), take a 60-90 second break and then decide if you would like to perform an additional round.

Tabata #7
Squat Jump
Push Up

Train and push your body to perform each exercise for 20 seconds at 100% effort followed by a brief 10 seconds of rest. Perform exercises back-to-back in a circuit fashion and perform the following exercises for 4 total rounds. Once you complete 4 rounds (4 minutes), take a

60-90 second break and then decide if you would like to perform an additional round.

Tabata #8
Russian Twist
Kickouts

Train and push your body to perform each exercise for 20 seconds at 100% effort followed by a brief 10 seconds of rest. Perform exercises back-to-back in a circuit fashion and perform the following exercises for 4 total rounds. Once you complete 4 rounds (4 minutes), take a 60-90 second break and then decide if you would like to perform an additional round.

Tabata #9
Kettlebell Swing
Kettlebell Squat

Train and push your body to perform each exercise for 20 seconds at 100% effort followed by a brief 10 seconds of rest. Perform exercises back-to-back in a circuit fashion and perform the following exercises for 4 total rounds. Once you complete 4 rounds (4 minutes), take a 60-90 second break and then decide if you would like to perform an additional round.

Tabata #10
Dumbbell Squat to Press
Mountain Climber

Train and push your body to perform each exercise for 20 seconds at 100% effort followed by a brief 10 seconds of rest. Perform exercises back to back in a circuit fashion and perform the following exercises for 4 total rounds. Once you complete 4 rounds (4 minutes), take a 60-90 second break and then decide if you would like to perform an additional round.

Tabata #11
Bench Dip
Band Pull Apart

Train and push your body to perform each exercise for 20 seconds at 100% effort followed by a brief 10 seconds of rest. Perform exercises back to back in a circuit fashion and perform the following exercises for 4 total rounds. Once you complete 4 rounds (4 minutes), take a 60-90 second break and then decide if you would like to perform an additional round.

Tabata #12
Plank
Superman

Train and push your body to perform each exercise for 20 seconds at 100% effort followed by a brief 10 seconds of rest. Perform exercises back to back in a circuit fashion and perform the following exercises for 4 total rounds. Once you complete 4 rounds (4 minutes), take a 60-90 second break and then decide if you would like to perform an additional round.

Tabata #13
Side Plank (Left)
Side Plank (Right)

Train and push your body to perform each exercise for 20 seconds at 100% effort followed by a brief 10 seconds of rest. Perform exercises back to back in a circuit fashion and perform the following exercises for 4 total rounds. Once you complete 4 rounds (4 minutes), take a 60-90 second break and then decide if you would like to perform an additional round.

Tabata #14
Blackburn

Superman

Train and push your body to perform each exercise for 20 seconds at 100% effort followed by a brief 10 seconds of rest. Perform exercises back to back in a circuit fashion and perform the following exercises for 4 total rounds. Once you complete 4 rounds (4 minutes), take a 60-90 second break and then decide if you would like to perform an additional round.

Tabata #15
Kettlebell Swing

Hands to Elbow

Train and push your body to perform each exercise for 20 seconds at 100% effort followed by a brief 10 seconds of rest. Perform exercises back to back in a circuit fashion and perform the following exercises for 4 total rounds. Once you complete 4 rounds (4 minutes), take a 60-90 second break and then decide if you would like to perform an additional round.

CHAPTER 7

Strength Training

If you have been training and practicing the fundamentals for 6+ months, this is another type of programming that we use for individuals who want to focus on strength while keeping fit and conditioning. Here are three of some of the best movements to develop strength throughout the body.

Barbell Squat

The king of lower body exercises, which strengthens and builds the quads, hamstrings, glutes, and core. Before starting the exercise, ensure that you have proper mobility by testing out your bodyweight and kettlebell squat technique. I have had many clients, including high-level athletes, who had hip and postural issues when performing the kettlebell and bodyweight squat. If you are unable to perform the other squat variations without compromising form, then I would suggest taking a few weeks off to increase your mobility and lower body strength.

If you are in the clear, the next step is to place the bar on your upper back and not your neck. Stand around shoulder width apart with your toes slightly pointing forward. Take a deep breath and engage your core as you descend. It is common practice to hunch our lower back and have our knees pass over our toes when squatting, but this will increase the risk of injury in the lower back and knees. <u>I highly recommend having a trainer or coach check out your form.</u>

Barbell Deadlift

If the barbell squat is the king of lower body exercises, then the barbell deadlift is the king of total body strength and building overall mass. Walk up to the bar and have your feet behind it shoulder-width apart. You may stand a little wider or narrower depending on your body mechanics and exercise feels. When you look down, the bar should be floating around midfoot.

Next, hinge and bend at the hips. While keeping a strong neutral spine, grab the bar just outside of where your knees are at. Take a deep breath and pull the slack out of the bar (you should hear a slight clicking sound). Then, drive your heels into the ground and extend your hips forward, lifting the bar off the ground. <u>With great reward also comes great risk. This is another exercise that I highly recommend having a trainer or coach watch your technique.</u>

Barbell Bench Press

Many powerlifters and bodybuilders see the barbell bench press as one of the best strength- and mass-builders in the chest. Avoid pressing with a 90-degree elbow angle, as it puts unnecessary stress on the shoulders. Keep your elbows tucked in around 45 degrees. Grab the bar just outside of shoulder width. By widening and narrowing the space between your hands, you will put more focus on either the chest (wider) or the triceps (narrower). Keep your feet on the ground and engage your glutes by driving your heels into the ground.

Basic Gym Equipment

If you have access to barbells, kettlebells, medicine balls, resistance bands, and a suspension trainer, you will love these workouts. I highly recommend that you have a professional or a seasoned coach go over your form for these next exercises and workouts. The exercises are very beneficial but also have a higher risk of injury if done incorrectly, such as the barbell squat and deadlifts.

Three Strength Training Sessions per Week

The reason why I highly recommend three strength training sessions per week for nearly all of my athletes and clients is because it is the amount that allows most people to have optimal results in terms of joint and muscle recovery. This is vital for longevity, hitting new personal bests, and feeling fresh coming into training. Most people already face stress from work, school, family, relatives, etc., and working out is another form of stress, which if not managed properly can make life more chaotic. Setting three days a week for strength training also gives you the ability to add cardiovascular workouts without over-training, if you would like to work out more often. By simply adding two high-intensity conditioning days, you have essentially created a 5-day workout plan.

Whether you are a beginner, intermediate, or advanced trainee, you will love this program. I have used variations of the following workouts for people of all backgrounds, from the stay-at-home parents to executive managers and collegiate athletes. These workouts are 100% customizable for you and your goal, and I will do my very best to guide you in the same manner as my private training clients to become your healthiest and strongest version. These workouts will have you building lean muscle, burning fat, improving blood markers, and increasing your cardiovascular system all at the same time.

In the following pages, I will be showing you multiple training programs and templates that have been the foundation for our clients. *Please note that this is not a one-size-fits-all program. I would be happy to help you at www.YanagidaFitness.com for a fully-customized program.*

Sample Training Template

If you are just starting out, and can only dedicate three training sessions a week, I totally understand. This is the sample structure I use for very busy clients.

Monday   — Strength (lower body)

Tuesday   — 30-60-minute walk

Wednesday — Strength (upper body)

Thursday   — 30-60-minute walk

Friday   — Strength (full body)

Saturday   — Outdoor activity/walk

Sunday   — Rest/active recovery

Warm Up and Mobilize

I highly recommend you do a thorough dynamic warm up as prescribed earlier and also add a mobility program. Include movements such as using a hip circle and walking forward, backward, and laterally for about 3-5 minutes to mobilize the lower body. Arm and shoulder rotation exercises, such as arm circles, band pull apart, face pulls, and band pushdowns done 15-30 reps, will greatly mobilize your rotator cuff and elbows and lower the risk of injury.

The strength portion of the workout is performed with rest periods of 1-5 minutes and should never be rushed to be completed. Always emphasize proper form and have a spotter if possible. The strength circuit portion of the workout is much different from the circuit-based workouts in the previous chapter. These circuits will increase your performance, strength, and heart rate.

Strength (Lower Body)
Barbell Squat Variation—Work up to a heavy set of 3-7 reps

Variations not limited to Front, Back, Back Squat, Box Squat, Bulgarian Split Squat, etc.

Start with a light weight and perform 5-10 reps. Then, gradually increase weight and decrease the reps as you get closer to your heavy set of 3-10 reps, e.g. empty barbell x 10 reps

*Note: This is not supposed to be a grinding, body-shaking-like-a-fish type of set.

Strength & Fitness Complex

Perform 2-4 sets

12 Kettlebell Swing

12 Stiff Leg Deadlift

12 Hands to Elbow

12 Back Extension

Perform each exercise and take as many rest periods as needed in between to complete the workout. Depending on your fitness level and goals, increase or decrease the repetition and the weights used in the circuit.

*__Note:__ Feel free to swap the exercises with others that meet your specific goals and needs.

Strength (Upper Body)

Barbell Press Variation—Work up to a heavy set of 3-7 reps

Variations not limited to bench press, close grip bench, overhead press, etc.

Start with a light weight and perform 5-10 reps. Gradually add weight and decrease the reps as you get closer to your heavy set of 3-10 reps.

*Note: This is not supposed to be a grinding, body-shaking-like-a-fish type of set.

Strength Complex

Perform 2-4 sets

12 Push up

12 Dumbbell Row

12 Dumbbell Shoulder Press

100m Farmer's Walk

Perform each exercise and take as many rest periods as needed in between to complete the workout. Depending on your fitness level and goals, increase or decrease the repetition and the weights used in the circuit.

*Note: Feel free to swap the exercises with others that meet your specific goals and needs.

Strength (Full Body)

Barbell Deadlift Variation—Work up to a heavy set of 1-5 reps

Variations not limited to conventional deadlift, sumo deadlift, trap bar deadlift, etc.

Start with a light weight and perform 5-10 reps. Gradually add weight and decrease the reps as you get closer to your heavy set of 1-5 reps.

*Note: This is not supposed to be a grinding, body-shaking-like-a-fish type of set.

Strength Complex

Perform 2-4 sets

12 Kettlebell Squat

12 Lunge

Plank as long as possible

100m Sprint or Sled Drag

Perform each exercise and take as many rest periods as needed in between to complete the workout. Depending on your fitness level and goals, increase or decrease the repetition and the weights used in the circuit.

*__Note:__ Feel free to swap the exercises with others that meet your specific goals and needs.

CHAPTER 8

Mentors and Coaches

Mentors & Coaches

I love being a student and learning from others, particularly those who have done it and continue to practice what they preach. I have many mentors for different areas of life, not limited to philosophy, fitness, business, sales, marketing, self-awareness, etc.

This section explains why I believe that to get ahead in life it is absolutely vital to reach out for help and receive advice from someone who has accomplished what you want. Sure, it's cheaper to do it yourself, but is it really? How much time is it costing you? When I first started doing my taxes for the business, I spent hours working on it and barely made a dent. I had a lot of uncertainty about whether I was doing it correctly, worries that only slowed me down. So, what did I do? I hired a CPA/ Bookkeeper. Those tireless hours trying to do my own taxes are now spent more effectively on other important tasks that I can work on myself.

This is where an ego check, humility, and implementation come into play. In reaching out for assistance, I do so with the understanding that there are certain things that others can do better than I can. The specified knowledge and experience that person can share could benefit my life and business tenfold. The same can be said with mentors and their advice. If I am not willing to receive and implement the help given to me, I will not be able to make a significant change, even if I have the best coach. Let's say you hire a coach to help you with your nutrition and get great tactics, strategies, and tips. However, you don't act on the advice and forget everything the coach tells you. What kind of results would you get?

Lessons from my grandfather

My grandfather, Naomitsu Nara, was born in Hokkaido and lived in a studio-sized room with seven siblings. His formal education stopped after middle school when he decided to enter the workforce, hoping to provide for his family by taking on many different jobs that ranged from mining rocks to singing to sales. However, he understood that education is important and was committed to reading books on topics that would help him in his work and in learning to associate with people that he looked up to.

He recalled that his most painful memories were not the physical labors, which in his time in Japan meant working from 6 a.m. to 6 p.m., but of times when he had to have his wife help him mine rocks to make ends meet after they got married. My grandmother is a very strong and capable woman, but he had decided that he didn't want to have her mining rocks all day with him. He committed to becoming a professional singer on Japan's biggest radio station, the NHK. Many people laughed, made jokes about him, told him it was impossible and that only the connected become a pro. He did not care what others thought except that he wanted to provide for his family.

It took him many tries and thousands of hours of practice and traveling before he reached his goal. He traveled and auditioned halfway across the country every single time to a different location only to fail 18 times in a span of two years with zero promise that he would actually become a professional singer. However, it didn't matter to him, as he was committed to finishing what he started. On the 19th attempt, he finally made his dream a reality.

Nearly a decade later, the radio stations were slowing down and cutting back on doing live broadcasts and shows, leaving my grandfather without a job for a few months. Then he stumbled across a poster that called for salespeople in his city. Without knowing anything about sales, he jumped in and made the commitment to become great at this, too, all with the intention of providing for his family. He started reading books and learning everything he could on sales, influence, persuasion, and how to really serve a customer. After many years and thousands of hours of dedication, he became the top salesperson in his city. He made it to his goal of getting into the middle class.

During my teens, my grandfather always told me that all we have is our word and that "if you say you're going to do something, then you must complete it no matter how difficult." Another favorite he told me was to always do what is necessary and challenging first. Lastly, he always reminded me to be humble, to learn from many people, and to never stop learning. He is a prime example and continues to read books, topics, and articles on health and faith at 91 years of age.

Key Points from Grandfather's Experience

- Commit to completing what you start.

- Self-education is very important.

- Don't waste time thinking about what others think.

- Our words must be matched by actions.

- If it is important, then do it every day.

My grandfather was one of my first mentors and I have learned and continue to learn from him as well. However, I have a handful of other mentors including Todd Durkin, one of the top trainers in the fitness industry who has made a profound impact on me.

Lessons from Todd Durkin

Todd Durkin, The Impact Man, father, husband, trainer and leader. I had known about Todd because he trains Drew Brees and other professional athletes, along with his reputation in helping other gym owners. The first time I ran into Todd I actually went to the wrong room and popped into his P10 mastermind meeting. The way he stood up, smiled and looked me straight in the eyes with a firm handshake, a gut feeling immediately told me he was the right person to connect with.

A few hours later, with many other fitness professionals, we showed up to his gym, Fitness Quest 10, and got after an epic workout together. It was full of energy, and inspiration and perspiration, to say the least. What he told me post-workout opened my mind. He asked me, "What made you fly over the Pacific Ocean to come here?" I initially said I wanted to improve procedures and systems in our fitness studio. He looked straight at me and asked, "Are you sure?" and, "Is there anything else?" I paused for a few seconds and then said that deep down, I also want to improve myself personally as a person, coach and improve my leadership skills and awareness to effectively add value and serve more people in our community. He told me that we, as individuals, can only go as far as we grow and that the little things count. From early morning to late evening sessions, every single high five, handshake, huddle, and conversation with people is vital and to never take that for granted. Over the last 20+ years many things have changed and evolved, such as workout styles, exercise equipment, heart rate monitors, wearable technology, etc. The one thing that has not changed and is still the foundation of what we do—he paused and looked at all of us trainers—and said the foundation remains the same, **relationships** and **genuine care** for others.

Over the next three days, we went over a host of different topics ranging from leadership, marketing, to being in the trenches. I highly recommend Todd Durkin's mastermind and coaching programs for anyone who wants to take their productivity, leadership, and career to the next level.

Key Points from Todd Durkin

- Leaders lead people through tough times.
- Change the mindset of "I have to" into "I get to"
- Sometimes we must slow down to speed up.
- "Get Your Mind Right"
- If it is important, then do it every day.

CHAPTER 9

Fitness or Sickness?

With all the people we helped go from being sick to fit, it is worth noting that many have parents and family members who have ill health or are overweight and obese. I can also tell you about clients who have very fit and healthy parents and family members while they alone are obese and have health-related issues. There is no such thing as an obese gene in the human body. As long as you have control of your eating and exercising activities, you will achieve and enjoy great health and fitness levels. Clients who were once 20, 50, and even 100 pounds overweight with unhealthy blood markers never blamed anyone else for who they had become. These people understood that nobody was forcing them to eat anything and that they were the ones constantly making choices. Choosing differently was also the key to changing their lives. The only way to attain great health and fitness is to take action and change our carefree mindset to that of healthy individuals.

1. Power of Habits

Habits are so powerful that they shape our lives for better or for worse. We all have bad habits, everyone, including your mentors, professors, parents, and friends. All we can do is replace the bad with a good habit. Being able to replace fast food with food that you already have made and is ready to eat will make the transition smoother. Going to a fast food drive-thru takes more time than you think. You have to leave the house earlier and wait in line, plus the 5-10 minutes it'll take to prepare your food. Conversely, if you had prepared food that just needed to be heated up for a minute, you would have saved time and stress on your part. Even if you don't like prepared meals, you could easily scramble up eggs with veggies and eat a piece of fruit within that 5-10-minute slot of going to get fast food.

Another great example is packing your workout clothes with you instead of returning home to change before heading to the gym. Many people in the past have expressed how much easier it is to skip a workout if they had to head home to grab their clothes. Being self-aware and auditing our actions is a surefire way to replace the bad with great habits. In the beginning, the habits will require discipline and willpower, and I recommend only changing one habit at a time until the new habit is characteristic and no longer requires effort.

2. Maintain a Positive Attitude

Individuals who maintain a positive attitude throughout their journey are much more likely to achieve their goals and constantly look for solutions even when things get tough. Having a positive attitude toward yourself, your workouts, and your nutrition program will reap more benefits than someone with a negative mindset, even if they have a superior workout and nutrition program. Having a positive attitude is also important for you especially if you have friends and family members who do not want you to change, as it will help you persist and stay strong. Simply tell these people that you would rather fail going toward your goals than be disappointed by not attempting your goal. Positive thinking alone has never helped anyone achieve anything, but it will propel you in the direction necessary and fuel the massive actions that you will be taking.

3. Embrace Challenges

Throughout your health and fitness journey, you will encounter many challenges, whether it be challenges of finding time to prep meals, workout, or even personal challenges such as family and work commitments. People who have successfully overcome major health issues typically embraced challenges as opportunities to improve and find better solutions. To achieve your goal of being healthy, you must see challenges as opportunities for growth. Not many people make changes or improvements when they are comfortable. Life can be unfair at times, but when you feel as though the world is preventing you from achieving your goals, remember that overcoming challenges will turn that experience into a tool that will move you closer to your goal.

4. Persist Through Plateaus

Being able to persist through plateaus and unexpected events and maintain your goal and course of actions is one of the most important traits for achieving your goal. This means that you will not lower your target because of setbacks or look for different solutions to attain them.

For example, when I was 19 years old, the doctors and medical professionals said that I would never be fit because of my liver, explaining how stress through exercise could possibly worsen it. However, that did not deter me from finding solutions on how to overcome my problems so that one day I could help others do the same. They had also told me that no matter what I tried with diet and exercise I would crash, unless I took to medication for the rest of my life. This plateau led me to great mentors who taught me many exercises and nutrition that would help me overcome the need for medication. Today, I have great blood markers and liver function with no medication.

When you hit a plateau in losing weight or increasing your strength, you have two choices—stay stuck and eventually quit, which is what the majority do, or persist and find a solution to your current problem. The way you eat and exercise when you are losing your first 5-10 pounds will most likely differ from the last 5-10 pounds that you would like to lose. Being persistent will not only be a great benefit for your health but also lead to success in many other areas of life.

5. Commitment to Completion

Anyone who has a high level of health and fitness has consistently committed to their goals. People who have a hard time making changes in their lives are usually the people who have difficulty committing to activities. They are the same people who will "try" to exercise and eat right, and most individuals only talk about trying but never get started. Commit to that one-year gym membership and find someone who will keep you accountable. Even if you do not know all of the details on how you will eat or exercise to achieve your goals, it is vital that you make up your mind to accomplish your goals no matter what. I would rather take clients who are fully committed over someone who is highly knowledgeable but flaky and bails out of their exercise and nutrition lifestyle.

Lately, commitment seems to be something many people shy away from, but looking back at anyone great, they all had this trait in common. I believe that without commitment we will always end up with average health, relationships, careers, etc., because we will most likely back out and change our minds when it gets difficult. Having firm conviction to do whatever is necessary is how to live a fit and full life. One of my mentors said to me, "If a baby is attempting to walk and continues to fall, when do you as the parent say enough, stop trying to walk, you'll hurt yourself? The answer is until they can walk."

6. Have an Open Mind

People who have great results had to change their approach to what they were doing in the first place. They might have changed their methodologies of eating and nutrition, such as going from eating six meals per day to doing intermittent fasting and then only eating two meals per day, or they might have adjusted their workouts, such as changing exercises of two hours a day, 6 days a week to 45 minutes, 3 days per week. For you to achieve a level of fitness you have never reached before, you have to have an open mind and a willingness to try new things. When I started working out, it was almost a no-brainer that you had to eat 6 small meals per day to burn fat. Now, there is research that illustrates the benefits of intermittent fasting and how only eating 2-3 meals per day gives similar, if not better, results so long as the daily calories, macronutrients, are equal.

I've had many clients who were fixated on thinking that running was the only way they would be able to burn fat and achieve the goals that they had set. They would go for months not losing any weight—some actually gained weight. After they accepted that they needed a different approach, we changed their regime. Eleven months later, they achieved their goal of seeing their six pack for the first time in their life and did so in a healthy, methodical manner. Keeping an open mind and learning new things is how you can overcome a hurdle in life, no matter how big and difficult it may be.

7. Maintain Massive Goals

When you first set your goal to go from having sick-to-fit blood markers, dropping 50 pounds to be back to your college weight, or even wanting to achieve a visible six pack, never lower your target. If people aren't doubting that you can achieve your goal, then it most likely is not big enough and will not fuel you through the challenges that you will face. The first thing that most people do when they hit a plateau is to lower their target. They keep repeating this habit until they end up quitting on their goal of being healthy, somehow justifying in their mind that they don't need to. When people say to set realistic goals, they are saying to set realistic goals for the timeline provided. It is not unrealistic for someone who has 100 pounds to lose to want to set their goals to have a six pack, nor is it impossible for the person on multiple medications to one day be completely healthy and off of all medications so long as they allow time for their goals. A tip I like to give that has worked for many people is to write your big goals down and stick it somewhere where you can read it every day, like in the bathroom or in front of your computer screen.

8. Take Action Every Day

No matter what happens in your day, it is vital to do something that will move you forward on a daily basis. Healthy and fit individuals take actions for their health no matter where they are and what they are doing. You can see it in their habits of parking further away from their destination so they can walk more, taking the stairs to burn more calories, grabbing the fruit over the donuts, and slipping in a quick workout at home if they have other commitments and can't make it to the gym. The people in my life who are unhealthy almost always talk about a plan to do something but never even take the actions necessary to start. Positive thinking and commitment are vital to achieving your goal. By also taking daily actions, no matter how big or small, you will move toward your goals and achieve them in time.

9. Never Get Comfortable with Exercise

As you embark on your journey to becoming your healthiest version, you will find that you will start getting comfortable with the exercises and programs that you have set. This goes back to the quality of having an open mind and that everything will work, but there is nothing that will work forever. When we first start walking or strength training, our bodies are not familiar with the movement and will have to expend more calories to complete the actions. One mistake people make is continually repeating a failed approach. It is not only frustrating but also demoralizing due to all the time and effort they are putting in. Don't get me wrong, if a workout or program is working for you, then there is no reason to change it. If there are no improvements, it may require just a slight modification in your exercise and nutrition that may speed up your process, such as running moderately to running intervals. You should not be changing your entire program every week for the sake of changing, only modifying areas that are not working. Eventually, you may need a partner or a group that will push you beyond your normal workouts, and it is not a shameful thing. Even the best athletes in the world (Olympic athletes) all have coaches that help push them beyond limits they never thought they could cross. Never get comfortable with your workouts and always strive to be a healthier and stronger version of yourself.

10. Motivation

Many people talk about motivation but are not able to say or explain what it is. Motivation is simply your motive for action, aka your "why." When people call me Mr. Motivation, they think I'm just a high energy coach, but what it really means is that I'm able to dig deep and tap into other people's emotional reasons for wanting to become healthier. For example, when someone tells me they want to simply lose 30 pounds, that is not their real reason for exercising. When we dig deeper, they will start to speak from the heart, presenting reasons such as wanting to fit into a nice dress after letting themselves go after a divorce. For some people, they might want to keep up with their kids or grandkids and live a long happy life with them.

Spending just a few minutes daily to embrace your "why" will propel you and give you the motivation to take action and persist through challenges and plateaus. Having a deep understanding and awareness of your why will be what separates you from all of the people that have attempted to get healthy and achieve their goal.

11. Have Discipline

In today's society, having discipline on exercises and watching what we eat are almost looked down upon. People will make you feel guilty and try to push their idea of not being disciplined as the way to go. I have met people who have said, "If my spouse and kids didn't take up so much of my time, then I'd be healthy." I truly believe that we should never use our family as an excuse as to why we are unhealthy and unable to reach our goals. They should be the reason why we want to live a healthier lifestyle.

12. Self-Care

While life is busy and the world tends to react to situations rather than act on them, don't forget to be proactive in taking care of yourself.

Mind: Feed your mind with positive, educational, and inspirational content, such as books, podcasts, conventions, etc. Even if you are busy and feel like you have no time, schedule time for those activities and commit to at least 15 minutes a day. Wake up 15 minutes earlier, use 15 minutes of your lunch break, or utilize your driving time to learn via listening to audiobooks or podcasts. 15 Minutes a day of reading = 15 books per year which in three years is equivalent to the number of books read for a PhD.

Body: Nourish your body through regular exercise, staying hydrated, and eating foods that give you the best energy, health, and vitality. The old adage of "an apple a day keeps the doctor away" is good advice. However, many people attempt to eat seven apples in one day instead, trying to make massive changes in a short period of time. This also applies to exercise. Completing an intense workout once will create a brief impact but not a lasting one. Start with something simple you can commit to first, such as walking your dog before/after work, doing yoga or zumba, or participating in a fitness class. If you're like our clients that have very busy lifestyles and feel like you have to pick one or the other, simply do both at once. Many people, including myself, will listen to audiobooks and podcasts while walking, jogging, or biking.

Spirit: Rejuvenate your spirit and get back to center. This is vital to living your best life, whatever that may look like to you. When we as a friend, parent, leader or teammate feel internally burnt out, we can no longer add value to those around us and can end up sabotaging ourselves and those around us. We believe our purpose and mission in life is the key differentiator in those who wake up jumping out of bed feeling and living with an abundant mindset, happiness, and fulfillment. Whether this is being of service to your community, blocking out time for your loved ones, going to the mountains/ocean or meditation, find what works best for you and commit to putting it in your schedule.

These are some common activities that indicate that our spirit may be burned out:

- – Addiction to alcohol/drugs

- – Addiction to sugar and fried foods

- – Habit of procrastinating

- – Comparing ourselves to others

- – Sensitive to other people's opinion

- – Enjoys gossiping, rumors and always sees the negative

- – Lack of empathy

- – Don't want to get out of bed

- – Worried rather than excited about the future

If you answered yes to any of these, don't worry. You are perfect and only a little off course and need to re-center.

13. Inspiration

When you are inspired, you are in spirit with your passion, purpose, or calling. Motivation is great and will last temporarily because it's something where you have to push yourself, but inspiration is when something pulls you towards something bigger than ourselves.

14. Be the Light

In today's world, many people see being positive or having high levels of energy as atypical. If someone asks you how you are doing, you might reply with a high-energy "I'm doing and feeling awesome!" Most people will react to that in their minds by thinking something along the lines of "What is this guy on?" or "He can't really be this happy, right?" or "This person is too much for me." Most of the time, they will walk away. On the contrary, if you tell someone you feel horrible, hate your job, or show disdain for something on the news, you will most of the time get agreement and be drawn into a conversation about how bad everything is.

Regardless of what people think initially, people are moved by emotion (energy in motion). It may take some time but continue to serve and add value to the people you see every day regardless of who they are and what they've said or done to you. We can all get caught up in our lives and forget to think if a person is acting and doing certain things because he or she is going through a challenging time. That's not to say we're justifying other people's behavior, but we don't have to take things personally and allow other people to sway how we feel.

My last takeaway is that I truly wish you to be a light in your community and maximize your gifts you have to share with the world by dialing into your best practices to get your mind, body, and spirit on fire to serve and make the world a better place.

"Darkness cannot drive out darkness; only light can do that. Hate cannot drive out hate; only love can do that."
—MARTIN LUTHER KING JR.

If any of the previous qualities we have discussed seemed daunting, then rest assured that all of them are learnable and applicable to everyone. I know that if you have read this far, you will achieve great success in your health and athletic and fitness journey. Also know that if you fall off the bandwagon from time to time, it is totally normal and happens to even the best of us. Just make sure you jump back on as soon as you can.

What's Possible

To show you some what is possible, I thought I would share some personal stories and life lessons from the staff at Yanagida Fitness.

Allyn Kalaiwaa

Intro:

Hi! My name is Allyn Kalaiwaa and I was born and raised on Maui. I'm currently a 4th grade teacher at Lihikai Elementary School, the Director of Operations at Yanagida Fitness, and a bartender/waitress a local bar. I'm pretty simple. My favorite things to do are nap, exercise, play video games, watch anime, hangout with my friends and family, and eat.

Life Story:

I don't necessarily remember much, but I feel that I had a pretty normal childhood. I was part of a family that was loving and supportive, even when my older brother, Lindsey, and I argued. We were always on the go with activities like sports, 4-H or Boy Scouts, and dance recitals. We'd spend a lot of time at our grandparents' house in Wailuku and our cousins Micah and Jenna would come over to play. Jenna and I weren't really into dolls, so we would be running around outside playing with our brothers. We would be there to support them at the many basketball games they had and that's where we formed lasting bonds with two families in particular, the Matsuis and Helles. I remember going to Well's Park after Lindsey's MYBL games to play tennis, goof around at the basketball court there, or run around in the park. Our parents were there for the drinks after. They would be "suckin' em up" in the parking lot while the four sets of kids would be running around. The Helles and Matsuis have been our closest friends ever since. They're practically family. No, they are family. Even now, almost 20 years later, we're still partying together. We just moved from a parking lot to a deck.

As an adolescent, not much changed. I was still involved with sports, swimming and water polo in particular. I wasn't anything outstanding, just average, but I learned a lot. I used to swim for Maui Gold Swim Team, which doesn't exist anymore, at Kokua Pool in Kahului. Thanks to the outstanding coaching staff, Coach Tyler Orikasa and his father, Coach Ray Orikasa in particular, I learned many life lessons and a lot about myself, good and bad. I learned that hard work and the belief in yourself is important in any aspect of your life.

Now I'm not talking about being full of yourself and being cocky, but to believe in your hard work, talent, and have a healthy sense of self-worth to reach your goals. You won't be the best you can be on just talent alone. You'll need to work hard, persevere, have grit, and visualize yourself achieving that goal. However, being humble, respectful, and a team player are just as important as being good. I learned those same values when I got to high school. I went to Kamehameha Schools Maui, where I swam and played water polo. Coach Jen Bullock, Coach Leo Delatori, and Coach Kevin O'Brien, as well as the faculty and staff at Kamehameha, instilled those same values that my club swim coaches did; work hard, persevere, and be humble. Like I said earlier, I was never the very best, just average, but that didn't mean I couldn't have goals. With the guidance and influence of the coaches I've had through the years from club swimming to high school, I was able to reach many of them. I wasn't going to be the top competitor at state meets, but I was going to make sure I helped our team qualify. I wasn't the fastest, strongest, or most talented water polo player, but I'm gonna make sure I stay with my man and leave it all in the water. I learned that even if you aren't the best, that doesn't mean you can't be your best.

I brought the values that I learned with me to college. I swam for a Division III school, Whitworth University, in Spokane, Washington. It. Was. Rough. I'd have to wake up in the wee hours of the morning to trudge in the cold and snow to practice for two and a half hours, shower, head straight to my first class, eventually eat, and hopefully nap between my other classes before heading to afternoon practice for another session. We'd have one morning off a week, sprint group was every Tuesday morning, and have Saturday practice as well. Honestly, I had a hard time balancing practices, making up work or tests for away meets, having a full credit load, and being away from home in a city where I was almost always cold, and it was almost always overcast. Rarely did the sun come out to shine in the winter. In college was really when I started to notice and reflect on my mental state and self-talk. Although I was taught to believe in myself, I was never really a confident person. I was always self-conscious of how I looked, acted, or things I would say. I never wanted to do or say the wrong thing. I never really talked about it with many people, but I got diagnosed with depression and anxiety in college. As I reflected upon what that looked and felt like, I realized that I battled with this through high school, too. The thoughts I was having and some ways that I handled things made more sense. More so in college I felt alone, constantly tired, had episodes of being so extremely angry at such trivial things, was impulsive, easily irritated, cried in my room, episodes of lying in bed, missing practice and classes, didn't want to socialize with my friends or teammates anymore, and not really understanding why. Some days, I would go to bed at 2:00 a.m., wake up at 6:00 p.m., eat, shower, brush my teeth, go back to sleep at 6:30 p.m., and wake up for practice the next morning and would still be tired and unmotivated. After realizing that I was slipping in my classes and I wasn't performing as I should've been in swimming, I sought help. Although my story is in this book now, I don't particularly like people knowing deeply personal things about me. I went to talk to one person, the school counselor. I saw her once a week for an hour for the rest of my freshman year and once every two weeks for two years after that. She had me take a few tests and she determined that I was showing symptoms of mild depression and moderate anxiety. She referred me to a psychiatrist so I could get another evaluation where I was prescribed anti-anxiety and anti-depression medication. Over the next three years I tried about four different combinations of medication until I found one that really seemed to work. So much so that I thought that I was "better," decided to play doctor, and took myself off my medication cold turkey. Bad move.

The anger episodes and bad thoughts came back, so I had to go back on my medication. It took me awhile to realize that it wasn't just me being overly emotional as many people think depression and anxiety is. I had to be reminded that it was an imbalance that I had. Being away from home, out of my element, and without much sun, seemed to amplify my symptoms more. I didn't have a proper coping mechanism; I kept everything inside and hidden behind a smile. There were moments where I thought of taking my own life, but being an overthinker, I thought about how that would impact my loved ones and I didn't want to put them through that, although I would go back and forth convincing and unconvincing myself that maybe their lives would be better without me, without the burden of me. After finally opening up to some friends, I realized that it wasn't the only option for me. There were times when it did feel like it was, but I had to remind myself that things get better. It may not be the next moment, hour, or day, but it does get better and you become a stronger person for it.

After college, I goofed around and partied for the summer. It was September and I realized that the school year had started, and I wasn't doing anything with the Elementary Education degree I earned at Whitworth. I figured it was too late to apply, so I looked for jobs on

Craigslist and Indeed. One of the ads was for a server at Watercress Sports Bar and Restaurant. I went in one day to apply, blocking off the whole day to apply for as many jobs as I could so that my odds of getting hired was better. I walked in, started filling out an application, and halfway through, Mama-San came in, asked me a few questions and asked when I could start. I jokingly said that I was free the rest of the day and she told me, "Good. You can start right now." I had to let my mom know I wouldn't be making it to dinner and that I got a job. At Watercress, you had to be a bartender, server, hostess, and busser all at the same time. Working there, I had long hours, but made new friends and had a new appreciation for people who work in the restaurant industry. They bust their butts and work for their money, so please, tip your waiters and waitresses nicely. A couple months into working at Watercress, I started substitute teaching and coaching high school swimming at my alma mater, Kamehameha Schools Maui. It was fun and awkward at the same time because the people that were once my teachers, were now people that I would work alongside with. Knowing that I worked at a bar, they would ask me about alcoholic drinks, and it was just weird. I really enjoyed connecting with my past teachers all while getting my feet wet as an educator. After my sub duties were done for the day, I would drive down to their pool for swim practice.

I was the assistant coach for Amanda Jimenez. I am a firm believer that everything happens for a reason. If I had never started coaching at Kamehameha with her, I wouldn't be teaching at Lihikai today. I found out through her that there was an emergency hire position they were trying to fill. I applied, went in for an interview, got hired, and the rest is history. I love what I do, I love the people I work with, and I love my kids (even on the more frustrating days). People ask me why I'm a teacher or a high school coach because I don't make a lot of money. Well, I do what I do because it's not about me, it's for the kids and it will always be. People always comment, "Oh, you're so lucky, you have breaks and summer off." To be honest, it ticks me off a bit. They don't see that we come in before school, stay longer than we're contracted to, take work home, and go to bed thinking about kids that aren't biologically ours. They don't see that we're going in on the weekends and during breaks. Or that we need to work summer school for the kids that need extra help and for us to earn a little more money, except that money usually goes back into supplies for our classrooms. They don't see that we constantly need to be on our toes and need to make quick decisions and those decisions can greatly impact a student in a drastically positive or negative way. They don't see that our hearts break for the kids who are having a rough time at home or the extra time we put in tutoring students. Now, don't get me wrong, I'm appreciative that we have these "breaks," and that school hours allow me to have other part-time jobs, but why does it warrant us needing other jobs to support ourselves and our families? I know I went on a little rant, but please be more considerate with comments about teachers and getting breaks, because we're working hard for your kids. We're either working during our breaks or enjoying the time off because we deserve some down time. We didn't become teachers for the money or benefits, we did it for the kids.

If you are currently an educator or a coach and are treating this important job as just a paycheck or for benefits, and I say this with love, please either reevaluate your love and devotion to your kids and this career, or please leave. I understand that teacher burnout is real, so find a way to take care of yourself (that includes your mental well-being) or find a new career that will make you happy again. Sometimes that means taking a year or so off from working with kids, switching it up, then maybe coming back again fresh and renewed. Okay, I'll get off my soapbox now.

In adulthood, I still need to remind myself of the same things; we all have good days and days where the world seems to be crushing down on you. I remind myself that I have family and friends that love me, a job that I love with coworkers that I admire, and that things get better. It may not seem like it in the moment, but it does. I still get random moments of, "If I just crash my car now, it can be over," but I am mentally strong enough now where I quickly kick that thought out. I think I've only told a few people; I'm not sure my parents even know. Well, I guess they do now.

Which brings us to today. Although I'm still not 100% confident in my abilities as an educator, I'm working to better myself, including my confidence, so that I can be the best teacher for them, not just in academics, but in life skills, too. Learning to persevere when things get rough, or to be generous with those around you, or to be okay with making mistakes is a part of life that we're going to learn how to properly deal with. School isn't just about learning how to read, write, or solve math problems, it's also learning how to work well with others, to communicate effectively, to be responsible, and to have grit; skills that will translate past schooling, but in the workforce and life as well. I'm no longer a high school coach, but I hope that I was able to positively influence those athletes in the four years I was coaching swimming and water polo. Kids, if you're reading this, I love you, I'm proud of you, and I'm so thankful I was able to be a small part of your life.

Now, I'm still considered a coach, but with a different focus and clientele. I officially met Justin at one of our friend's mom's funerals, of all places. We chatted for a bit, then a little while later I got word that he started up his own local gym. He didn't have any morning classes and I couldn't make it in the afternoon because I had high school practices to coach. My friend, Tiffany, and I asked Justin to start a morning session for people who couldn't make the afternoon class. The morning session consisted of only three, sometimes four, people: Tim, Tiff, and me. Sometimes it would only be two of us. The workouts were different back then—dare I say easier? At the time, though, they seemed challenging and I was waking up sore on many occasions. I enjoyed it, though. I appreciated Justin's energy and dedication to those around him. I stuck around, started going to afternoon classes as well once high school season was over, and one day Justin asked if I would consider being a coach and leading classes at the gym. Being the insecure person that I was, I naturally thought he was joking or asked the wrong person by accident. I was taken aback and a bit flattered, honestly, that he was serious about making me a coach. So, I took the certification course and was a part of the first group of coaches under Justin. I started shadowing him, observing how he motivates others, and tried to follow his lead. Eventually, I was solo coaching classes and the rest is history. The gym's motto "Fighting Sickness with Fitness" can mean many things to different people. To me, the motto can mean more than lowering your cholesterol or losing weight. It also speaks to mental health and self-talk. I'm not saying that working on your mental health means you're sick or something is wrong, I'm saying that you end up loving yourself more and your confidence and self-worth grow. At Yanagida Fitness, you gain a family that supports you throughout your journey. We're all in the same boat, myself included. We're all working to be a better version of ourselves, whether that's physically, mentally, emotionally, or spiritually. Justin has created a safe space where we can be ourselves and progress toward our goals together. He's really created and built something truly special. I'm thankful to be a part of his journey and this family.

Three Life Lessons:

1. Everything happens for a reason. As I mentioned earlier, I'm a firm believer that our lives play out in a certain way for a purpose. The things we experience,

good and bad, make us who we are. The people that have come into our lives, even if it seemed like only a brief moment, have helped shape our life experiences. I often think about if I hadn't done this or if I hadn't gone to that, I wouldn't have met some amazing people or even be where I am or who I am today. Though we experience loss and heartache, I've learned that it's necessary. It teaches us how to cope, how to communicate, how to love, and to know what you deserve. It's taken me a while, but I've learned that even though we may call something a mistake, it's not really a mistake. It's just a lesson for us to experience and learn from. It's a life lesson. And when we make the same "mistakes" over and over again, and we get hurt time and time again, it's life trying to shove that lesson into our thick skulls until we learn and understand that we deserve to be happy. It'll take some work on our end, too, though, so be ready to work at it.

2. I know it may seem contradictory of my first life lesson, but if you're unhappy, then do something about it. If we go through the cycle of choosing the same path, getting hurt, but doing the same thing again and expecting to get a different result without changing anything, we'll go through the loop endlessly. You need to make a conscious effort to want something better and do what's

best for you. It's a vicious and destructive habit. We continuously complain about something, like maybe a job that you say you hate, but aren't putting in the work to find a different job, you'll go through this vicious cycle and it takes a toll on your mental and physical well-being until you choose to change it. Nothing is going to improve until you choose to do something about it. To quote one of my favorite Instagrammers, Luucybee (go follow her!), on my favorite video of hers to date (pardon the language), "Heartbreak is a motherfucker, but so is wasting time, so dry your eyes … get up, get dressed, get pretty, and go fuck some shit up! Live, baby!"

3. Self-care is so incredibly important. I've only recently learned this. Make time for yourself to unwind. For me, that looks like watching anime or a drama series, taking a nap, going to the gym, or going out to dinner or drinks with my friends. For you, it might be meditating, going for a swim, cuddling with your pet, or getting your nails done. Whatever it may be, make time for yourself. Many of us make time for everyone else and make sure that they're happy, while we put ourselves last. Although it's good to put others before yourself and be selfless, you're important, too. Read that again, YOU'RE IMPORTANT, TOO. Schedule time to treat yourself. Take a bubble bath, immerse yourself in a book, take a walk; do something

for yourself. Mental health is essential. "You can't pour into a cup if the pot is empty." Take time to re-energize. You matter, too.

3. "Fun" Facts About Me: One, I've been fortunate enough to have travelled to eight other countries. Some were in high school on spring break trips in association with the Spanish Club. Others were part of a cruise ship trip when I was in elementary or middle school while I was dancing for Skipper's School of Dance (may she rest in peace). Thanks to my parents, I've had the opportunity to travel as much as I have. Others have traveled more than me and that's fine. We didn't have a huge excess of money, but my parents made it work to provide my brother, Lindsey, and I with life experiences. I'm thankful and so appreciative of all the opportunities I have had the privilege to experience so far.

Two, growing up, we always ate at Grandpa Fuj and Grandma Grace's house every Monday. Besides *natto* (fermented soybeans), one of my favorite foods was hot rice and Grandpa's "special" *ikura* (salmon roe). One day, my parents got a call from my elementary school. They said that I was acting really odd. I was lethargic, easily agitated, and it seemed like I wasn't feeling very well. My grandparents lived down the road from my school, so my grandpa picked me up from school and piggybacked me to their house where I spent the rest of the day napping. I didn't have a cold, a fever, or anything. They thought about what it could've been that made me that way. Come to find out, my grandpa soaks his "special" *ikura* in *sake* (rice wine). My parents speculate that I overate the *ikura* and had a baby version of a hangover the next day. Ever since then, they regulated how much of grandpa's "special" *ikura* I could eat at a time on a school night.

Three, I have four tattoos right now, five if you count my permanent makeup as well. The first tattoo I got was my permanent makeup before I started college. I got my top eyeliner and my wetline done. It wasn't too bad, but my eyes are sensitive, and I kept twitching. I haven't been maintaining the darkness, so I add a bit of eyeliner to my everyday makeup. However, it's nice to wake up and have some makeup on to walk out the door. I know it sounds vain, but it helps me feel just a bit less insecure.

My other tattoos have actual meaning to them. My second tattoo is on the inside of my left wrist. I got it in April 2014 during my senior year at Whitworth University. While attending Kamehameha Schools Maui, we were taught pillar Hawaiian values. One that stood out to me was *ho'omau* which means to persevere or perpetuate. Realizing and living with depression and anxiety, I really clung to ho'omau. I wanted a visual reminder that when life is throwing me through constant loops and keeps knocking me down, I persevere and trudge on. I tried to preach ho'omau to my high schoolers when workouts were tough, when we were behind in points, or when morale was low. I think that it's important to be mentally tough and not give up so easily. Hopefully that transcended to the kids. Even as a classroom teacher and a fitness coach now, perseverance is a "soft skill" that is so incredibly important to learn, kids and adults alike.

My third tattoo is on the side of my right wrist. I got it in February 2016. It's a semicolon. People ask me, "Why do you have a punctuation mark on you?" I basically explain the gist of 'Project Semicolon' which was founded in 2013 by Amy Bleuel, that, "a semicolon is used when an author could've chosen to end their sentence but chose not to. The author is you and the sentence is your life." It's become a symbol for mental health and suicide prevention. One of my best friends, Tiffany Matsui, and I went to get this tattoo together. She has been one of my biggest supporters for many years and shoulder to lean on when I have felt my weakest. She gives me her honest opinion and will tell me the truth, even if I don't want to hear it. Without her, I'm not entirely sure that I would be here to live the life that I have so far. Without her, I would not be who I am or where I am now. And for that, I can never thank her enough.

My fourth tattoo is on my back. It's my mother's maiden name in Kanji as well as our family crest. The Kanji was done October 2018 and I added the family crest in July 2019. Family means a lot to me and when my maternal grandfather, Fujio Shibano, passed away, I was devastated. He was the first person close to me that had died. I still remember that day. I had just finished coaching water polo practice and was just heading out to go to my grandparents' house for our Monday dinner. We've been going to their house for dinner on Mondays for as long as I can remember. I got a text from my cousin Jenna and she was giving her condolences for my grandpa. I immediately called her and asked her what was going on. Grandpa Fujio had passed away in his sleep at home. I was crushed and angry at the same time. Why didn't anyone call me before? Did it happen before practice? Were there signs that this would be his final day? Could I have said goodbye? Why didn't I spend more time with him? All these thoughts and feelings rushed through my head as I talked with Jenna for 20 minutes all the way from practice to my grandparents' house. I'm thankful that she was able to stay on the phone with me as I tried to fight tears while I was driving. When I got there, an ambulance and police car were outside the house. When I saw him lying on the bed, I sobbed for a long time, then became angry and wanted an explanation as to why I found out through text. Well, I'm the emotional one in the family. Things weren't looking good earlier that day, but they didn't want me to worry and distract me from my duties as a teacher and as a coach. They also didn't want me driving alone when I found out. I was driving by myself anyway when I received that text, but because of Jenna, I was able to hold it together long enough to drive safely. I knew that my parents withheld that information for my safety, but I was still upset and had a hard time accepting what had happened. Fortunately, though, I was able to say my last goodbye before the coroner took him away. We'd always exchange our goodbyes with "See you later, alligator," so as I watched them roll him away, I whispered back with a lump in my throat, "In a while, crocodile. Love you." Jenna's late Grandpa Tom and my late Grandpa Fujio were brothers. Uncle Tom was an amazing calligrapher while Grandpa Fujio was great with crafts. Uncle Tom wrote the kanji for Shibano and drew our family crest on a wooden plank while Grandpa Fuj carved it out. It still hangs on my grandparents' porch. In July 2019, Jenna and I went together to get our tattoos. This was her first tattoo and she was nervous. I brought her to Jun at Fathom Deep Tattoo because he did my kanji the previous year and he was very good. He makes you feel comfortable and less stressed. I highly recommend him. She got the kanji tattooed on her ribs while I finished my back piece with our family crest. I wanted to make sure that Jenna and I went together. We've helped each other through our grandpas' deaths, and we will be there for each other through more life events, both happy and sad. We're family, after all.

My fifth tattoo, I got in May 2019; exactly a month after my first (and currently only) fur baby's death. I was and am still feeling the loss of our dog, Lyla Fukagawa. She suddenly passed on April 23, 2019 from a sudden mesenteric tear that caused a huge part of her intestines to become septic. Dr. Weeks and Dr. Camara at Maui Lani Veterinary Hospital told us that her intestines that were twisted were so black and putrid, it was amazing she even made it on the surgery table, let alone through the whole thing. Lyla has had health issues before and has always overcame them. We'd pick her up from the vet, tail wagging and giving the best kisses. You'd never have known she was sick in the first place. We have been fortunate to have had Dr. Weeks, Dr. Camara, and their staff taking care of Lyla. We were extremely hopeful that she'd pull through yet again and things were looking up, so her dad, Josh, and I went to the clinic to transport her to a 24-hour-care facility post-surgery. When we arrived at the clinic past their usual closing time, an awful odor hit us at the door and filled the room as we waited to see Lyla. They rolled her out on a cart so that we could take her to a night clinic to recover. As she became more aware as the anesthesia started to wear off, I noticed that she was crying. She had tears coming from her eyes as I walked closer to see her for the first time right after surgery. Now that I look back on it, it was like she knew she didn't have a lot more time with us, that this was going to be it; this was her saying goodbye to us. We put her in my backseat with Josh holding up her IV bag as it slowly dripped. The 24-hour-care animal clinic was only five to ten minutes away from where we were. "We can make it, Lyla. Hold on, baby. Please." I thought to myself as I got in the driver's seat. Halfway there, Josh noticed the IV bag stopped dripping. He asked me to drive faster. We parked at the clinic. It's about 10:30 p.m. at this point. No one is at the front desk. I looked around corners to find someone, anyone. Finally, a nurse came out and I let her know the situation. She went to my car, checked Lyla's heartbeat with her stethoscope, and said she needs to go get the vet. At this point, I started to realize what that meant; she didn't have a heartbeat.

I started to go into a panic and crying hysterically. My heart was broken, absolutely crushed. The only fur baby I have ever had and with the expectation that we'd have her for many years instead of only a little more than a year and a half, I was devastated. I don't bawl very often, but I felt like I lost my child, my own flesh and blood. I couldn't help but cry out in anguish as my tears flowed like raging rivers from my eyes. I'm so thankful to have had Josh there with me. I knew he was hurting too, but he remained much calmer as he broke the news to his parents and tried to get ahold of our vet. He continued to console me, sob after sob, tissue after tissue. We weren't prepared to say goodbye forever. A week or so had passed and my mom had mentioned that her massage therapist said that oftentimes, if their owner is in danger, out of love, they'll die in their owner's place. This broke my heart even more. The night Lyla started to get sick (the night before she died), I attended a blessing at the school I work at. When the *kahu* and his wife arrived at our classrooms' wing, she asked the three of us that were there from our wing if we have had major health issues in the past couple years. All of us had. Most recently, I had an appendectomy a few months prior and catheter ablation for my heart three days before the blessing. His wife can sense, and she said that the *ali'i* (chief) that was there was trying to take one of us out; that if the blessing wasn't done, one of us would have died by the end of the year. In my mind, Lyla died protecting me. She did what I could never repay her for. In Hawaiian culture, *ti* leaves are a symbol of protection. I asked Jun, the tattoo artist who did my family crest and kanji, if he could sketch something with ti leaves, Lyla's name, and a dog paw print. I wanted to honor her in the most permanent way I knew how. He drew up a beautiful sketch and exactly a month after she passed, I got her tattooed on my left rib cage, close to my heart. I know that she protected me and continues to protect me even after crossing the rainbow bridge. We finally buried her in 'Iao Valley on Josh's family's property on July 20th, 2019, on what would've been her second birthday. We didn't have as much time with her as we anticipated, but I hope she lived a life where she knew she was loved and cared for. Rest in love, Lyla girl. Daddy and Mommy miss you, but we love you and you'll be with us in our hearts forever.

I haven't quite figured out what my next tattoo will be, but I know that I want to honor my dad's side of the family. Kalaiwa'a in Hawaiian means master canoe builder and our *'aumakua* (family god/protector) is a *mano* (shark). That's all I have as of right now. Shhhhh, don't tell my mom! She doesn't like tattoos. Sorry (not sorry), Mom!

Other:

Thank you to my mom and dad for teaching Lindsey and I how to work hard, persevere, and to be caring to others. We know that you folks have sacrificed a lot for us, and we want you folks to know that we appreciate all that you do. Love you!

Tyler Hultquist

Intro:

My name is Tyler Hultquist, and I was born in Maui, Hawaii. I am currently 27 years old and work as a lot attendant at a car dealership. I recently started working with Justin as his Assistant Manager/Head Coach for the gym.

Life Story:

I had a great childhood filled with lots of friends. I will say that there were a lot of things that I never knew about the world. For example, I didn't even know cell phones existed until one of my friends brought a yellow Nextel to school and we all thought it was a walkie talkie. Growing up, there were a lot of things that I would question, especially when things didn't make sense to me. It bothered me when instead of explaining something, people would tell me that I just had to listen, or that this was just the way the world worked. That never really made any sense to me. In school, my favorite subjects were math and science. While I loved math, it always bothered me that I had to show my work when I could easily do it in my head. I tried to show my teachers that I already knew what I was doing, but they told me time and time again that I had to show my work in order to prove that I wasn't cheating or using a calculator. School soon became boring, and I started receiving lower marks. Intermediate school was a little better, but I was still frustrated with school. I never took my frustrations out on people, but I was always taking it upon myself because I wasn't getting the best grades. No one could really give me a reason as to why my grades actually mattered. I already knew at that age that a lot of the stuff I was learning wouldn't apply in my life. It felt like such a waste of time. In 7th or 8th grade, I told one of my friends that I could not figure out the reasons for why I was born, how everything worked, and why I had to learn and do things the way people wanted me to. Would I be spending the rest of my life just listening to people and having to do what they told me to do? I bottled up those emotions and felt like there wasn't a good enough reason for the things I was doing at the time. Yet, I was kind-hearted and wanted to help the people that needed my help. In high school, I was a teacher's assistant and helped my classmates. It was funny, because even though I was placed in a lower level math class, I could still help my classmates who didn't understand math. I surprised one of my teachers with how I completed certain tasks. What was straightforward and simplistic to me was different for them. My teachers deemed me "not good enough" and kept placing me into the lower classes. I just looked at things very differently when it came to certain subjects.

I lived my life going with the flow, letting people, to a certain degree, control what I did growing up because that's what was expected of me. I cared more about what it meant to be a person than learning about information and how to use it. I believe that teaching a human being about how to be a human being is more important than teaching them information from a book that they may or may not use in the future. I want to help people become who they were always meant to become, not someone that people expect them to be. If we force people to do what they don't want to do, there's no happiness, and that's one of the biggest things that any individual on this planet could ever want. Happiness is one of the most important things that you can give a person.

Fighting Sickness with Fitness:

Fighting Sickness with Fitness means exactly what it says. I'm always straightforward and to the point, and that's why I love this. Fighting Sickness with Fitness is using exercise and diet to fight your own illness. However, that's just one part. That's why I feel like this place is going to do a lot more down the line. Right now, even if it's just the gym, I see it could be so much more. Fighting Sickness with Fitness is just a part of three pillars that are paramount to the human condition. One pillar is the physical body, having a healthy body that allows you to do things you want and need to do to effectively survive and thrive. Another pillar is the mental condition. Being understanding and seeing things through other people's perspectives are important traits in connecting with people. The last pillar is the soul or a person's emotions. Having control over your emotions can be difficult but is also important in maintaining a healthy soul. Sometimes, sickness of the body can be easier than repairing the sickness of someone's mind or the sickness of someone's soul, but all three pillars need to stand together to work. There's always more that we can do as coaches, teachers, and human beings. We can be healthier, have more energy, more conditioning, pick up more weights, have more control over our emotions, or have more empathy for someone else. I feel that as time goes on, we as a gym will go deeper into these things, where we not only help people physically but also mentally and emotionally through fitness, exercise, knowledge, compassion, and understanding.

Life Lessons:

Try to understand as much as you can from another person's perspective, regardless of their decision-making or emotional outbursts. You may not understand why somebody's having a bad day or why the person on the road just cut you off. That's the point, though. We don't know exactly what the other person may be going through. Without perspective, you only see things from your point of view, and that's only one way of seeing things.

Pass on knowledge and wisdom, because we don't do that enough. Teach people how to be better human beings. We expect our children to just figure things out sometimes, and that never made sense to me growing up. How can you expect a child to understand something that they have never experienced?

Practice empathy, kindness, love, and acceptance. We need to be more kind, more caring, more understanding, and have more empathy, not only for your family and friends, but also for the people you've never met before. Whether it is the person walking down the sidewalk or the person randomly scrolling through your social media that you have never talked to before, it doesn't matter. Just be kind.

Fun Facts:

I can do the most monotonous, simplistic, repetitive thing over and over again without getting bored. For example, I can sit and watch all the sand in an hourglass fall or doodle on a piece of paper with the same pattern over and over again until the paper is full only to throw it away and start again. Normally, these sorts of things keep my mind busy, but it can also be fun even if it might seem boring to others.

I am always willing to listen to anybody that wants to speak to me because sometimes people just want to be heard, and sometimes listening is enough. I am always there if someone needs my help and always try to be a friend. I will try to make others feel that they can trust me and that if they needed somebody to have their back, I had it.

I'm also flexible enough to put my leg behind my head. Is that fun? Not really. Is it a fact? Sure.

Goals in Life:

One goal of mine is to spend a portion or majority of my life doing the best I can to give back. I want to gather as much as I can, whether it is monetary wealth or knowledge, and share it with others. Nothing we have is permanent, regardless of what we think it is. We might as well spend most of our lives giving back as much as we possibly can.

Another goal is to make people happy. If I had happiness, that's all I would ever really need. Happiness can sometimes seem in short supply, and therefore my second goal would be to provide as much happiness in other people's lives as I can.

The third goal is to help people break past their limitations. If they would allow, I would gladly motivate from the sidelines, push them from behind, or pull them by the hand. I'd even carry them if they needed to, but they would have to allow me to do it in the first place. I also want to help people help others. By helping someone through their tough times, that person can in turn help another person, creating an infinite cycle that could do more than any of us could imagine. One simple act of kindness or compassion, even if it's just a sentence, can change the entire outcome of history.

Closing Words:

Find the thing that makes you happy. Find that thing that genuinely brings you joy and happiness and do it for the rest of your life. That alone would probably bring you all the happiness you could ever ask for.

Stephanie Riglos

Intro:

My name is Stephanie Riglos. Most people know me by my maiden last name, Crisologo, and call me Steph or Stiphie (a high school nickname). I was born and raised on the island of Maui. I am extremely clingy, so I've never learned to leave my family for long. I am married to my husband, Jim, and have four French bulldogs, Deux, Toro, Penelope, and Mia. I am currently the Assistant Director of Finance for Montage Kapalua Bay, and I coach at Yanagida Fitness when I have some free time.

Life Story:

I basically live life on the fly and do what I can, as much as I can, daily. I like a very structured and scheduled lifestyle, as I'm extremely predictable. But I do like a good adventure when time permits, and I seem to never be satisfied. I do like a good push and challenge, but at the same time, I know my limits and sometimes can get in my own way, if that makes any sense.

Fighting Sickness with Fitness means to me to do anything I can possibly do to keep a healthy and active lifestyle year-round. This also includes bringing others along with me for the ride.

Life Lessons:

Life lesson one—you want something, get up and get it. Nothing comes without putting in the actual work.

Second life lesson—if something doesn't work, move on and find another route.

Life lesson three—live life to its fullest. I try to take nothing for granted, as each second comes and goes. There is no way back and regrets are solely on myself. Each step I take forward, whether good or bad, is taken with gratitude and as a lesson for future steps. Everything I do is a choice taken upon myself, and I am solely accountable for all of my actions.

Fun Facts:

Call me an introvert, yet, if you get to know me, you can't shut me up.

I get hangry very easily. I'm always hungry and I'm a complete junk foodie.

I can't cook to save my life, but I'm the best food taster. But did I mention I'm extremely picky?

I can honestly say I'm at a point in my life where I am content. I would like a human child of my own, possibly in the next two years, but not in a rush. Ain't nobody trying to give up any sleep any time soon. I would prefer not having to schedule my life around my job and have a job where I just clock in and clock out at the end of each day, but I've worked hard to be where I am today and I'm not quite ready to give that up yet. My current goal is to travel out of the country at least twice a year and to other places I have yet to see closer to home throughout the year. Other than that, just living life on the fly and making it all count each day.

Yasss girl, get it! Do you, boo. <3

Taylor Hovious

Life Story:

I was born and raised on the island of Maui, you know, lucky live 808. My mom and dad raised me until I was five, then my grandparents took over and have raised me ever since. My life was just like every other kid; I had good friends who were close to my family. However, I also had a lot of hardships and stress. When you're a kid and you experience all of these different difficulties, you really have a hard time understanding what's going on.

Growing up, I was a shy but angry kid who would blow up in a lot of situations. The outbursts only got worse as I grew up, but at the same time things were still good. I had two great-grandparents who always provided me with whatever I needed. Then when I was twelve, my grandfather passed away suddenly. Cancer took him quickly, and my grandmother raised me from then on all by herself.

Graduating from high school with a 3.0 GPA, I was never really the type to try in school. I was always the "I'll just get by" type of person and cruised on. I attended the University of Hawaii, Maui College first then UH Manoa, where I really started to change. I wanted to do better, so I studied hard, working to get a degree, get out of there, and start doing something for myself. I graduated in May 2015 with a 3.7 GPA in the field of psychology. Six months later, I was in the National Guard. I lived on the mainland for a year doing things ranging from using a variety of military equipment to learning customs and courtesies. It was rough and very stressful, but it was fun.

During that time, I got to see my father's side of the family, who came to visit me when I graduated as an officer. I last saw them in Florida when I was ten years old. After my year of training, I returned home and started doing my thing; got hired by Whole Foods to start making money and lived life. In December of 2017, I became a fitness coach for Yanagida Fitness. Now, I am a Care Coordinator at Imua Services, Human Resources Officer for the National Guard, and fitness coach at Yanagida Fitness.

Three Fun Facts:

First, I love cats. I used to have 13 of them. That was a crazy time in my life. If a cat walks by, I'm going to stop what I'm doing to play with it, no matter what.

Second fun fact—I am a huge anime nerd. If we talk about anime, it is going to be a long conversation and we are not going to get anything done. Dragon Ball Z, YuYu Hakusho, and Cowboy Bebop are some of the few I enjoy.

Third fun fact—I am a huge running guy. I participated in track and cross-country in high school and got into marathon running when I was in my first two years of college. I did it just to enjoy it and had a blast during those years. If you ever have questions about cardio, then I'm your guy.

Three Goals:

My first goal in life would be to live as good of a life as I can. That's all we can really ask for, to be able to do things that make us grateful for what we have every day.

My second goal in life is to teach others, to help others become their best. I've always enjoyed teaching others and helping them. It really brings me a lot of joy when I see them improve and develop.

My third goal in life is to at one point do a Spartan Race. That's one of my things I want to do, but if not that, I would like to see another Dragon Ball series come out again. If I live to 70 or 80 and they come up with a new one, then life is good. I can die happy.

To me, "Fighting Sickness with Fitness" means doing your best to get rid of all the negativity in your life. We all get sick, we all have negativity in our lives, but if we try hard, give it our all, then we can start to reduce the negative, maybe even stop them, and be our best selves.

Three Life Lessons:

The first life lesson is not to take things so seriously all the time. I used to do that, and it really drains you and makes you see things in a negative light a lot of the time. Take things as they come.

The second lesson is to never look at something from one point of view. If you don't look at things from different angles, you'll never see the beauty of the situation and you'll never see it from another person's angle. It's kind of like art; if you and another person look at it, you're both going to see very different things, so try to have that open-mindedness to see things from all angles.

The third lesson is to try new things. Always try new things. That's the one thing I learned the hard way in life. I always like to stick to my patterns and my routines, but it's the new things in life that challenge us and make us realize like, wow, I didn't know I could do this. My example would be the military. Going into basic training, I never thought I could do that until I got there. Once I was finished, I didn't really think I had it in me, but I surprised myself.

Carol Kurisu

Life Story:

I was born and raised on Maui and lived here until I moved to Oahu after graduating high school to attend business school. I then met my husband, got married, and had two children. After 24 years of marriage, I divorced and returned to Maui to live with my parents. I am currently retired and live alone in my parents' home. I exercise at Yanagida Fitness and am now one of the coaches. I love my cats and dogs and enjoy racing my dad's 1993 Nissan.

I have always been quite an active person, running the 10th Honolulu Marathon, a half marathon, and a few 10K fun runs. After moving back to Maui, I continued to walk and did aerobics and Zumba. After a while, I knew that walking was not enough. I walked longer distances but did not see any promising results. I started looking at CrossFit gyms but knew that that was not for me. The workouts were geared towards the younger crowd with no flexibility for seniors. Then I found Yanagida Fitness through a mutual friend, and it has turned out to be wonderful. Justin is the greatest coach, the most supportive, and is so full of energy. Now, I'm a coach. He's contagious!

One of my goals in life is to be comfortable in my own skin. "Fighting Sickness with Fitness" has helped me to relax. I have become a stronger person physically and mentally, and I'm hoping that it helps to slow down the aging process, just a little bit. There are lots of people who flatter me because they can't believe how old I am. My renewed energy allows me to fulfill one of my other goals, which is to be healthy so I can travel and care for my pets.

Life Lessons:

1. Think twice before you do anything. Sometimes you need to think it three times.

2. If it feels good, then do it (but think twice).

3. Live for today because tomorrow is not promised.

Final Thoughts

Thank you for taking the time to read this book and for allowing me to share a part of my life with you. I am rooting for you and looking forward to hearing your success story.

If you would like to continue to connect with me, please follow me at:

Instagram—Justin_Yanagida

Facebook—Justin_Yanagida

Email—YanagidaFitness@gmail.com

Made in the USA
Las Vegas, NV
10 November 2020